50 WALKS IN

Scottish Highlands & Islands

50 WALKS OF 2–10 MILES

Contents

WALK		RATING	DISTANCE	PAGE
1	CRUACHAN	+++	2 miles (3.2km)	10
2	IONA	+++	5.25 miles (8.4km)	13
3	INVERARAY	+++	4 miles (6.4km)	18
4	INVERARAY	+++	6.75 miles (10.9km)	23
5	ISLE OF MULL	+++	8.25 miles (13.3km)	24
6	LOCH RANNOCH	+++	3.75 miles (6km)	26
7	GLEN TILT	+++	6.5 miles (10.4km)	29
8	LOCH FASKALLY	+++	8.75 miles (14.1km)	32
9	PITLOCHRY	+++	9.5 miles (15.3km)	37
10	KINLOCH RANNOCH	+++	2.25 miles (3.6km)	38
11	GLEN COE	+++	2.75 miles (4.4km)	40
12	GLEN COE	+++	8 miles (12.9km)	43
13	KINLOCHLEVEN	+++	3.5 miles (5.7km)	46
14	KINLOCHLEVEN	+++	6.75 miles (10.9km)	49
15	INCHREE	+++	2.75 miles (4.4km)	50
16	STRONTIAN	+++	7 miles (11.3km)	52
17	NEVIS GORGE	+++	2.5 miles (4km)	55
18	BEN NEVIS	+++	10 miles (16.1km)	60
19	COW HILL	+++	7.25 miles (11.7km)	63
20	CORPACH	+++	4.5 miles (7.2km)	64
21	COIRE ARDAIR	+++	8 miles (12.9km)	66
22	FORT AUGUSTUS	+++	7.25 miles (11.7km)	69
23	BRAEMAR	+++	6.75 miles (10.9km)	72
24	BRAEMAR	+++	5.5 miles (8.8km)	75
25	BALMORAL	+++	4.75 miles (7.7km)	76
26	GLENLIVET	+++	6.25 miles (10.1km)	78
27	LOCH AN EILEIN	+++	4.25 miles (6.8km)	81
28	GLENMORE	+++	5 miles (8km)	84
29	GLENMORE	+++	6.5 miles (10.4km)	87
30	BOAT OF GARTEN	+++	5.75 miles (9.2km)	88

AA

50 WALKS IN

Scottish Highlands & Islands

50 WALKS OF 2–10 MILES

First published 2003
Researched, written and updated 2009
by Ronald Turnbull
Reprinted February 2010

Commissioning Editor: Sandy Draper
Senior Editor: Penny Fowler
Designer: Tracey Butler
Picture Research: Susana Vázquez Fernández
Proofreader: Jennifer Wood
Cartography provided by the Mapping
Services Department of AA Publishing

Produced by AA Publishing
© AA Media Limited 2010

Published by AA Publishing (a trading
name of AA Media Limited, whose
registered office is Fanum House, Basing
View, Basingstoke, Hampshire RG21 4EA;
registered number 06112600)

  This product includes
mapping data licensed
from the Ordnance Survey® with the
permission of the Controller of Her
Majesty's Stationery Office. © Crown
Copyright 2010. All rights reserved. Licence
number 100021153.

A04395

ISBN: 978-0-7495-6292-2
ISBN: 978-0-7495-6325-7

A CIP catalogue record for this book is
available from the British Library.

The contents of this book are believed
correct at the time of printing. Nevertheless,
the publishers cannot be held responsible
for any errors or omissions or for changes
in the details given in this book or for
the consequences of any reliance on the
information it provides. This does not affect
your statutory rights. We have tried to
ensure accuracy in this book, but things do
change and we would be grateful if readers
would advise us of any inaccuracies they may
encounter.

We have taken all reasonable steps to ensure
that these walks are safe and achievable
by walkers with a realistic level of fitness.
However, all outdoor activities involve a
degree of risk and the publishers accept
no responsibility for any injuries caused to
readers whilst following these walks. For
more advice on walking safely see page 144.
The mileage range shown on the front cover
is for guidance only – some walks may be
less than or exceed these distances.

Visit AA Publishing at theAA.com/shop

Cover reproduction by Keenes
Group, Andover
Printed by Printer Trento Srl, Italy

Acknowledgements
The Automobile Association would like
to thank the following photographers,
companies and picture libraries for their
assistance in the preparation of this book.

Abbreviations for the picture credits are as
follows: (t) top; (b) bottom; (l) left; (r) right;
(c) centre; (AA) AA World Travel Library.

3 AA/J Smith; 9 AA/J Smith; 14/15 AA/D
Forss; 20/21 AA/K Paterson; 22 AA/A
Hutchinson; 25 AA/A Hutchinson; 34/35
AA/J Smith; 57 AA/A Hutchinson; 58/59
AA/S Day; 65 AA/A Hutchinson; 80 AA/A
Hutchinson; 86 AA/A Hutchinson; 96/97
AA/S Whitehorne; 109 AA/A Hutchinson;
112 AA/A Hutchinson; 115 AA/A
Hutchinson; 116/117 AA/J Beazley; 126
AA/A Hutchinson; 133 AA/S Whitehorne;
140 AA/J Henderson;

Every effort has been made to trace the
copyright holders, and we apologise in
advance for any accidental errors. We
would be happy to apply the corrections
in the following edition of this publication.

Author acknowledgement
Ronald Turnbull thanks the following for
their help and advice: John Ireland, Forestry
Commission; Peter Duncan, SNH Craig
Meagaidh; Ordnance Survey Press Office;
Glyn Jones, Balmoral Estate; Priscilla,
Charlie, and Fiona Rose, Alligin; Margaret
at Grantown Museum and many others
who answered emails or were patient
on the phone. The paths in this book
are provided and maintained by many
organisations, including Atholl Estates,
Crown Estates at Glenlivet, Flowerdale
Estate, The Footpath Trust (Dingwall),
Forest Enterprise, Highland Council,
Inveraray Estate, John Muir Trust*,
Kinlochleven Land Development Trust,
The National Trust for Scotland*, Perth
& Kinross Council, Raasay Social Services,
Rothiemurchus Estate, Scottish Natural
Heritage, The Scottish Rights of Way and
Access Society*, Upper Deeside Access
Trust. Join one of the organisations
marked with an asterix to help fund
their future work.

Right: River Avon and the Cairngorms, Cairngorms National Park (Walk 26)

Contents

WALK		RATING	DISTANCE	PAGE
31	GLENELG	✚✚✚	8.5 miles (13.7km)	90
32	GLENBRITTLE	✚✚✚	5.75 miles (9.2km)	93
33	QUIRAING	✚✚✚	5.25 miles (8.4km)	98
34	QUIRAING	✚✚✚	5.75 miles (9.2km)	101
35	GLENBRITTLE	✚✚✚	5.25 miles (8.4km)	102
36	RAASAY	✚✚✚	7.75 miles (12.5km)	104
37	PORTREE	✚✚✚	3.5 miles (5.7km)	107
38	RAMASAIG	✚✚✚	5.75 miles (9.2km)	110
39	RAMASAIG	✚✚✚	5.25 miles (8.4km)	113
40	SHIELDAIG	✚✚✚	3.25 miles (5.3km)	114
41	STRATH CARRON	✚✚✚	9 miles (14.5km)	118
42	LOCH TORRIDON	✚✚✚	9.5 miles (15.3km)	121
43	GAIRLOCH	✚✚✚	5.25 miles (8.4km)	124
44	GAIRLOCH	✚✚✚	7 miles (11.3km)	127
45	BEINN EIGHE	✚✚✚	3.5 miles (5.7km)	128
46	POOLEWE	✚✚✚	6.5 miles (10.4km)	130
47	LOCH NESS	✚✚✚	4.25 miles (6.8km)	134
48	STRATHPEFFER	✚✚✚	10 miles (16.1km)	137
49	STRATHPEFFER	✚✚✚	5.5 miles (8.8km)	141
50	INVERNESS	✚✚✚	7 miles (11.3km)	142

Rating

Each walk is rated for its relative difficulty compared to the other walks in this book. Walks marked ✚✚ are likely to be shorter and easier with little total ascent. The hardest walks are marked ✚✚✚ .

Walking in Safety

For advice and safety tips see page 144.

Locator Map

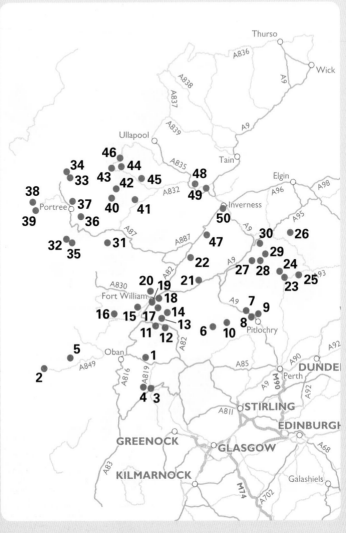

Legend

→	Walk Route		Built-up Area
①	Route Waypoint		Woodland Area
– – –	Adjoining Path	🚻	Toilet
☼	Viewpoint	P	Car Park
•	Place of Interest	开	Picnic Area
⌂	Steep Section	)(	Bridge

6

Introducing the Scottish Highlands & Islands

The mountains of Scotland come in various shapes. There are the green friendly fells of Perthshire, where the great River Tummel winds idly in its oak-tree gorge and salmon flash in the pools of Killiecrankie. There are the grim crags of Glen Coe – oppressive and even scary on days of low cloud, wind and beating rain. When the clouds do lift and the sun comes out, it's still oppressive and scary because you can see just how high they go.

Northwards we come into the Cairngorm massif. These hills are huge but rounded, where the plover cries like a bewildered soul above the fields of boulders. Down around the feet of the Cairngorms the great forest grows, once haunted by bears and wolves, brigands and fairies and broken men. It's tamer today, with red squirrels and tourists with their flasks and sandwiches. Again a great river flows through it, on a bed of golden shingle.

And so we reach the wilds of Wester Ross, where the sea runs in among the mountains. A wide, golden beach, a cragged headland, an ancient dun, and, out in the bay, the swift gleam of a porpoise – or was it a whale? After 18 hours of daylight the sun goes down behind a jaggy horizon that has to be the Isle of Skye. Skye, where the bog is boggiest, the midges are mightiest and the pointy purple mountains rise into a blue sky. (Or don't, because the cloud's down – so simply hop across to gentle Raasay.)

In those heather glens of the Grampians, and the green glens of the west, lived a people whose tribal lifestyle was basically Iron Age right up until the end of the Jacobite Rebellion in 1746 (see Walk 38). The clansmen have left behind their castles in the lochs and their summer huts high on the flanks of the hills. Above all, they've left their often sad stories: Glen Coe and Culloden, Rob Roy and Bonnie Prince Charlie, and Fingal who roamed the mountain tops before the start of history and played leapfrog across the Glenelg narrows.

Today we have it easy. When it rains, we put on our waterproof jackets and when it snows we go home. Nobody's going to descend out of Rannoch with a broadsword to murder us and steal our cows. But in a way it's the same old story – of pride and poverty, of the fierce love of the home hills. Instead of claymore and fire, the instruments of plunder are the bulldozer and the planning application. Hordes of humans versus the natural world – it's as fundamental as Highlander versus the King in Edinburgh or London.

PUBLIC TRANSPORT

The Highland railway lines are among the most beautiful in the world – but, apart from the main line north to Inverness, the service is slow and infrequent (Scotrail – National Rail enquiries 08457 48 49 50; www.scotrail.co.uk). There is, however, a very useful coach service (Scottish Citylink 08705 50 50 50; www.citylink.co.uk) from Edinburgh and Glasgow to Glencoe, Fort William and Skye. Local buses and postbuses run once a day up many of the glens (www.travelinescotland.com, 0871 200 2233), while frequent CalMac ferries run to Mull, Iona and Raasay (www.calmac.co.uk).

In this book you'll find a couple of summits – but mostly these are the coastal walks, the forest walks, the walks that go around instead of up the hills, or through the passes, or along the great rivers. Even so, the paths here are harder than in the rest of Britain. Some are peaty trods, unchanged since the days of the cattle drovers. The way will be more tiring than you think, and the higher and longer ones need to be treated with respect (see Walking in Safety on page 144).

And if your feet are in a bog – though mostly these walks are chosen so they won't be – who cares? The rest of you is in the bleak or leafy, the sea-beaten, crag-hanging, faery-haunted Highlands of Scotland.

Using this book

Information panels

An information panel for each walk shows its relative difficulty (see page 5), the distance and total amount of ascent. An indication of the gradients you will encounter is shown by the rating ▲ ▲ ▲ (no steep slopes) to ▲ ▲ ▲ (several very steep slopes).

Maps

There are 30 maps, covering 40 of the walks. Some walks have a suggested option in the same area. The information panel for these walks will tell you how much extra walking is involved. On short-cut suggestions the panel will tell you the total distance if you set out from the start of the main walk. Where an option returns to the same point on the main walk, just the distance of the loop is given. Where an option leaves the main walk at one point and returns to it at another, then the distance shown is for the whole walk. The minimum time suggested is for reasonably fit walkers and doesn't allow for stops. Each walk has a suggested OS map in addition to the map in the book.

Start Points

The start of each walk is given as a six-figure grid reference prefixed by two letters indicating which 100km square of the National Grid it refers to. You'll find more information on grid references on most Ordnance Survey maps.

Dogs

We have tried to give dog owners useful advice about how dog friendly each walk is. Please respect other countryside users. Keep your dog under control, especially around livestock, and obey local bylaws and other dog control notices.

Car Parking

Many of the car parks suggested are public, but occasionally you may find you have to park on the roadside or in a lay-by. Please be considerate when you leave your car, ensuring that access roads or gates are not blocked and that other vehicles can pass safely.

Right: Loch an Eilein, Rothiemurchus Estate, Cairngorms National Park (Walk 27)

The Hill with the Hole

Looking along Loch Awe from Cruachan Reservoir,
Britain's biggest energy storage system.

DISTANCE *2 miles (3.2km)*   MINIMUM TIME *1hr 45min*

ASCENT/GRADIENT *1,200ft (365m)* ▲▲▲   LEVEL OF DIFFICULTY +++

PATHS *Steep rugged paths, 2 ladder stiles*

LANDSCAPE *Wooded slopes and high corrie*

SUGGESTED MAP *OS Explorer 377 Loch Etive & Glen Orchy*

START/FINISH *Grid reference: NN 078268*

DOG FRIENDLINESS *Good, but high and steep ladder stiles to negotiate*

PARKING *Two pull-ins on north side of A85, below railway station.*
Also lay-by 0.5 mile (800m) west. Not visitor centre car park

PUBLIC TOILETS *Cruachan Visitor Centre*

The Cruachan Reservoir collects rainfall from a fairly small catchment, 9 square miles (23sq km) bounded by the rocky ridge of Ben Cruachan. Even with Cruachan's 116in (2,945mm) of rain a year, only 4 megawatts of power are generated, not enough to supply Oban, to the west.

The Big Battery

But Cruachan is more than just a rather small power station. It's a rechargeable storage system for electrical energy, a very big electric battery. The demand for electric power varies from day to day, and even from minute to minute. There's the surge at the advertising break during your favourite soap, as a million kettles get switched on at once. Coal and oil power stations can be stoked up or cooled off, but only quite gradually. Nuclear stations run at the same rate day and night. And the greenest energy sources, wind and wave generators, give power according to the weather. So there has to be a way of taking electricity out of the National Grid when there's too much, and putting it back when it's most needed.

Cruachan Power

Fortunately, an electric generator running backwards becomes a motor, and a turbine turns into a pump. At 'white-meter' (off-peak) times of day, water is pumped from Loch Awe up to Cruachan Reservoir, 1,000ft (305m) above. And at 7:15 on a weekday evening, it flows back down again.

The stored energy in the battery of your car is sufficient to keep it running for about half a minute, but that's enough to start it in the morning and run the CD player when the engine's off. Full to the brim, Cruachan Reservoir, with the capacity of about half a billion car batteries, in theory holds enough potential energy to supply the UK's peak demand for 10 minutes. In fact the water can't be drawn down that fast, but at full flow Cruachan can supply 400 megawatts, enough for most of Glasgow. Time your arrival for 7:15pm, and you could see the reservoir sinking at an inch (2.5cm) per minute. The same amount of water will be flowing out into

CRUACHAN

Loch Awe, just beside the visitor centre. The whole process – pumping up and then retrieving the potential energy – is not much more than 50 per cent efficient. The waste heat ends up in Loch Awe, where it benefits the fish farm opposite the visitor centre.

The Secret Source

The Cruachan powerhouse makes a fairly small impact on the outer world. Around 12 miles (19.3km) of pipes bring water into the reservoir, and the outgoing or incoming electricity loops across the hill on high pylons. The 1,030ft (314m) dam is only visible once you reach the corrie; the power station itself is actually buried deep in the heart of the mountain.

WALK 1 DIRECTIONS

❶ Two paths run up on either side of the Falls of Cruachan. Both are initially rough and steep through woodland. The western one starts at a tarred lane opposite the entrance to the power station proper (not the visitor centre, slightly further to the west). This diminishes to a track, which becomes rough and crosses the railway as a level crossing. A path continues uphill in steep zig-zags through birch, rowan and oak. There are various points

WHERE TO EAT AND DRINK

There's a café at the Cruachan Visitor Centre during its opening hours. Oban has a wide selection of cafés, restaurants and pubs looking out over the harbour. The Falls of Lora Hotel, at Connel Bridge, has a bistro offering everything from fish and chips to venison and oysters (no dogs allowed). Watch out for Loch Etive's seals and otters opposite to the hotel.

to stop and admire Loch Awe, which disappears glittering in the distance. White speckled stones in the path are Cruachan granite. The path continues on steeply to the top of the wood.

2 Here a high ladder stile crosses a deer fence. With the stream on your right, continue uphill on the small path to a track below the Cruachan dam. Turn left, up to the base of the dam, which measures 1,030ft (314m) wide and 150ft (46m) high. Because it's tucked back into the corrie, it can't be seen from below, but it is clearly visible from the top of Dun na Cuaiche (see Walk 3), 12 miles (19.3km) away. The hollows between the 13 huge buttresses send back a fine echo. Steps on the left lead up below the base of the dam, then iron steps take you on to the dam's top.

3 From here you can look across the reservoir and up to a skyline that's slightly jagged at the back left corner, where Ben Cruachan's ridge sharpens to a rocky edge. In the other direction, your tough ascent is rewarded by a long view across Lorn. Turn right to the dam end, where a track leads down right to a junction, then right for 50yds (46m).

4 At this point you could stay on the track to cross the concrete bridge just ahead, leading to the top of the path used for coming up. Otherwise there is a clear path as you go down to the left of the stream, to reach a high, steep ladder stile. (There's a useful dog flap in the deer fence alongside.) Below this there is a clear path that descends grassy slopes and gives a good view of some of the Falls of Cruachan. Inside the wood, the path becomes steep and rough for the rest of the way down. Just above the railway, it turns left, then passes under the line by a low tunnel beside Falls of Cruachan Station, to the A85.

WHILE YOU'RE THERE

From the visitor centre, you can pass by underground tunnels to the vast chamber of the Machine Hall, which houses the power station's four turbines. At this point you're about 0.75 mile (1.2km) into the mountain, and 1,000ft (305m) below the reservoir. Waste heat from the turbines, as well as plenty of electricity for lighting, means that subtropical plants are able to thrive in this technological underworld.

WHAT TO LOOK OUT FOR

From the mountain slope you look down the length of Loch Awe to its distant outflow – except that you don't. Loch Awe is a reversed lake. Since the ice age, the original outflow at the southern end has silted up and raised the water level to the point where a new outlet formed at the north-western corner. As the descent from here to the sea is fairly steep, a small gorge has formed. This has lowered the lake level and eliminated the original outflow altogether.

The Holy Island of St Columba

A circuit of Iona to the marble quarry and the saint's landing place in Coracle Bay.

DISTANCE 5.25 miles (8.4km)   **MINIMUM TIME** 3hrs 30min

ASCENT/GRADIENT 650ft (198m) ▲▲▲   **LEVEL OF DIFFICULTY** +++

PATHS *Tracks, sandy paths, some rugged rock and heather*

LANDSCAPE *Bare gneiss rock and Atlantic Ocean*

SUGGESTED MAP *OS Explorer 373 Iona, Staffa & Ross of Mull*

START/FINISH *Grid reference: NM 286240*

DOG FRIENDLINESS *Keep on lead near sheep*

PARKING *Ferry terminal at Fionnphort on Mull*

PUBLIC TOILETS *Beside Martyr's Bay Bar*

In the early summer of AD 563, a middle-aged cleric crossed over from Ireland with 12 companions and the intention of setting up a monastic community on the remote and windswept island of Iona.

Flight of the Dove

Columba (in Gaelic, Colum Cille, 'the Dove of the Church') did not intend to bring Christianity to a new country, indeed he had left his native Ireland under a cloud. It had started with a dispute over copyright: Columba had secretly copied a psalter owned by St Finnian of Clonard, and Finnian had claimed ownership of the copy. The dispute became more complicated when a young prince accidentally killed an opponent during a game of Irish hockey and claimed sanctuary with Columba. A battle followed, for which Columba felt responsible. In penance for these events he accepted 'white martyrdom', perpetual exile.

Irish Poetry

At the centre of Columba's settlement on Iona was a church of oak logs and thatch and, around it, huts for the individual monks. Columba himself slept on the bedrock with a stone for a pillow. Larger huts of wattle were used as the dining hall, guest house, library and writing room. The monks' lives consisted of prayer, simple farming and study, and here Columba composed poetry in Latin and Irish.

Celtic Calendar Calculations

Columba's Celtic Christianity spread from Iona across Scotland, and led to the Northumbrian foundation of Lindisfarne, with its rich tradition of illustrated documents such as the Lindisfarne Gospel. Here it came into contact with the Roman-style Christianity of continental Europe, brought to England by Augustine in AD 597. While the outward dispute was on the correct hairstyle for monks and the way to calculate the date of Easter, it seems that the Celtic Christianity was more personal and mystical, the Roman more authoritarian. The Roman version eventually dominated, but

Overleaf: Across Martyr's Bay to Iona Abbey (Walk 2)

the Celtic was never suppressed. Columba, never officially canonised as a saint, is venerated in Scotland and Ireland to this day.

Iona Today

Columba's church vanished beneath a later Benedictine abbey, itself heavily restored in the 19th century. But the spirit of Columba still dominates the island. From the low hill called Dun I, on the day of his death, he blessed the island and community. The monks grew kale and oats at the machars (coastal lowlands) of Bay at the Back of the Ocean (Camus Cuil an t-Saimh), over what is today the golf course. At the southern tip of the island is Coracle Bay, traditionally named as the saint's landing place.

'That man is little to be envied, whose patriotism would not gain force upon the plain of Marathon, or whose piety would not grow warmer among the ruins of Iona,' said the renowned English writer and critic Samuel Johnson, who visited the island in 1773. Today's Iona Foundation is ecumenical – tied to no single denomination of Christianity – and has restored the buildings within a tradition of simple craftsmanship and prayer. The grave of John Smith, Labour leader in the 1990s, lies in the north-east extension of the burial ground.

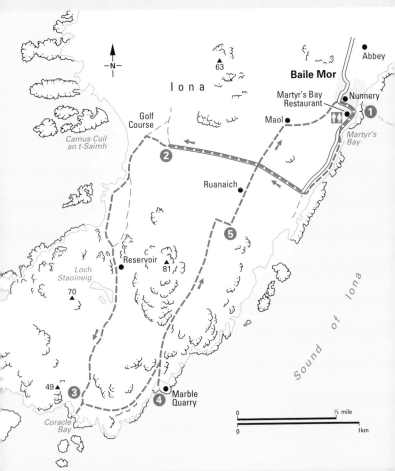

IONA

WALK 2 DIRECTIONS

❶ Ferries cross to Iona about every hour. Once on the island, take the tarred road on the left, passing Martyr's Bay. After a second larger bay, rejoin the road as it bends right. Follow the road across the island to a gate on to the Iona golf course (dogs on leads).

❷ Take the sandy track ahead, then bear left past a small cairn to the shore. Turn left along the shore to a large beach. At its end, bear left up a narrow valley. After 100yds (91m) you pass a small concrete hut to join a stony track. It passes a fenced reservoir and drops to the corner of Loch Staoineig. Walk along to the left of the lochan on a path, improved in places, that runs gently down to Coracle Bay. You cross to the left of an area that shows the furrows of lazybed cultivation – fields drained to improve crop yields – and reach the shore just to the left of a rocky knoll.

WHERE TO EAT AND DRINK
On the island, you can try the Martyr's Bay Restaurant, which offers fresh local seafood (March–November; dogs on the patio only). For a quick snack there's the Heritage Tea Room within the confines of the abbey.

❸ Take the route ahead following an indistinct path. If your ferry to the mainland leaves in 2 hours time or earlier, return by the outward route and leave exploring the marble quarries for another visit. Otherwise, return inland for 200yds (183m) and bear right into a little grassy valley. After 100yds (91m), go through a broken wall and then bear slightly left, past another inlet on the right. Cross heather to the eastern shoreline of the island. Bear left, above the small sea cliff, for 0.25 mile (400m). Turn sharp right into a little valley descending into the remnants of the marble quarry.

WHILE YOU'RE THERE
From Iona, or Fionnphort at the Mull end of the ferry, you can take a boat trip to Staffa to visit the legendary Fingal's Cave and its weird basalt formations.

❹ Turn inland, back up the valley to its head. Pass the low walls of two ruined cottages and continue in the same direction for about 200yds (183m) to a fence corner. Keep the fence on your left, picking a way through heather. Dun I with its cairn appears ahead – aim directly for it to reach the edge of fields, where a fence runs across ahead. Turn right along it to a small iron gate.

❺ This leads to a track that passes Ruanaich farm to the tarred road of the outward walk. Cross on to a farm track, which bends to the right at Maol. It reaches Baile Mor (Iona village) at the ruined nunnery. Just ahead is the abbey with its squat square tower, or turn right directly to return to the ferry pier.

WHAT TO LOOK OUT FOR
The shingle at Coracle Bay has cairns built by penitential monks. Over the years they have been renewed by visitors. Here you'll find greenish-white lumps of Iona marble among the grey gneiss. A long mound in the grass above the beach is supposed to indicate the dimensions of Columba's boat – 100ft (30m) long.

Climbing to the Castle of Cups

*Dun na Cuaiche offers a fine view of Inveraray,
Campbell capital of Argyll.*

DISTANCE 4 miles (6.4km)	**MINIMUM TIME** 2hrs 15min
ASCENT/GRADIENT 900ft (274m) ▲▲▲	**LEVEL OF DIFFICULTY** ✦✦✦

PATHS Clear, mostly waymarked paths, no stiles

LANDSCAPE Steep, wooded hill, some rocky outcrops

SUGGESTED MAP OS Explorer 363 Cowal East

START/FINISH Grid reference: NN 096085

DOG FRIENDLINESS Must be under control, not necessarily on lead

PARKING Pay-and-display, Inveraray Pier

PUBLIC TOILETS Inveraray Pier and Castle

Inveraray is the seat of the Duke of Argyll, chieftain of Clan Campbell. Thus it became, in the eyes of Campbells anyway, the capital of the southern Highlands.

The Campbells Have Come

Until about 1600, the main power in the Highlands was MacDonald, Lord of the Isles. The Duke of Argyll aimed to take his place – by the normal methods of intrigue and armed attack on neighbouring clans, but also by collaboration with the legal government in Edinburgh and the King in London. Clan Campbell would hit you with fire and the sword, but also with a writ from the Privy Council. As a result they became the most powerful and the most universally disliked of all the clans.

In 1691, King William demanded an oath of loyalty from the rebellious Highland chieftains. MacIan of the Glen Coe MacDonalds was required to sign his oath in Inveraray. He hesitated over this visit to the capital of his hated rivals, and eventually arrived two days after the deadline. His delay was made the pretext for the Campbell-led Massacre of Glen Coe (see Walk 11). When a Campbell was murdered in Appin 60 years later, the suspect, James Stewart of the Glens, was tried at Inveraray before a jury of Campbells, with Argyll himself as judge. The hanging of Stewart, who was almost certainly innocent, is still resented in the MacDonald country.

Argyll Rebuilds

With the breaking of the clan system in 1745, Argyll felt confident enough to pull down his fortified castle and rebuild in a grand residential style that suited a wealthy landowner who no longer needed to resort to violence to keep control over his lands.

The present building, greatly admired by Sir Walter Scott, is described as a country house in the style of a castle. Its grey stone, quarried from just above the town, is sombre, but tones well with the muted green and blue of the Campbell tartan. To go with his new castle, Argyll decided he needed a new town. Some say that old Inveraray was simply too close to the castle.

INVERARAY

But in its present position, curved around its bay, it's a magnificent and early example of a modern, planned town. It is dominated by the Court House where James of the Glens stood his trial, and by the white arches of the Argyll Hotel. One of these arches is a passageway for the A819.

The Duke of Argyll completed his ambitious rebuilding scheme with avenues and bridges; one of the bridges forms an elegant entry to the town on the A83. This walk crosses the Garden Bridge, designed by John Adam (1721–92) of the Scottish family of architects. The whole layout of castle and town is seen from the summit of Dun na Cuaiche (Castle of Cups).

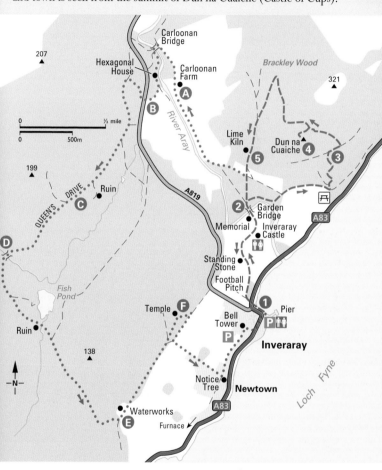

WALK 3 DIRECTIONS

❶ Follow the seafront past the Argyll Hotel and bear left towards Inveraray Castle. At the first junction, turn right past a football pitch with a standing stone. After the coach park on the left and the end wall of the castle on the right, the estate road on the left is signed 'Dun na Cuaiche Woodland Walks'. It passes a memorial to clansmen who were killed for religious reasons in 1685. Cross the stone-arched Garden Bridge to a junction.

❷ Half right now is the uphill path with coloured waymarkers that will be the return leg of

LOCH RANNOCH

Proper Forest and Granny Pines

As you reach Point ❹ of this walk, your spirits should suddenly rise. You have passed from what the Forestry Commission calls a forest, where trees destined to become pulp for paper stand trunk to trunk in grey gloom, to emerge under a more open canopy, where views are wide and where sunlight reaches the pine-needle floor and brightens the undercover of bilberry and heather. The cheerful reddish bark complements the dark green of the foliage above.

Here and there you'll come across an old pine that's too twisted to be of any use in shipbuilding, which has been spared – a so-called granny pine. The lifespan of a pine is 300 years or more, so these trees will have seen the last of the wolves pass by, and sheltered broken men after Bonnie Prince Charlie's failed rebellion in 1746.

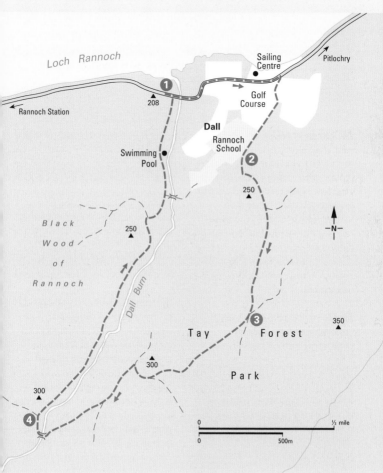

WALK 6 DIRECTIONS

❶ From the pull-in, walk back along the road with Loch Rannoch on your left and Rannoch School on the right. You pass its

commando climbing tower on the right, its sailing centre on the left and its golf course. At the former school's goods entrance, a Scottish Rights of Way Society (SRWS) signpost points up to the right –

this is an old and unused through route to Glen Lyon. Follow the tarred driveway past tennis courts to the first buildings and turn left at another SRWS signpost.

WHILE YOU'RE THERE
The first exploiters of the Caledonian forest were the Caledonians themselves: Iron Age Celts of 2,500 years ago. A unique insight into their lives can be found at the Scottish Crannog Centre at Kenmore, beside Loch Tay. Here you can walk through a reconstructed lake village built on pinewood stilts driven into the loch, which shows what life was like thousands of years ago.

❷ A sketchy path runs up under some fine birch trees. At an empty gateway in a decomposing fence it enters spruce trees and becomes a narrow track that's a little damp in places. Avoid a lesser path turning off to the left; the main one becomes a pleasant green path contouring across the slope with glimpses of Loch Rannoch on the right. The path runs up to a wide forest road.

❸ Ignore the path continuing opposite and turn right, contouring around the hill. Clear-

WHAT TO LOOK OUT FOR
A low, star-like flower below the birches at the walk's start could be mistaken for the common wood anemone, but is actually chickweed wintergreen. It can be identified by the rosette of leaves halfway up the flower stem. Most flowering plants die back in autumn to allow them to escape the frosts and winds, but on the sheltered forest floor, evolution has programmed this plant to keep its leaves through the winter — hence the name.

felling has opened up views to Loch Rannoch and the remote hills beyond. The highest of these, with a steep right edge, is Ben Alder, the centre of the southern Highlands. This hill is glimpsed from many places, notably the A9 at Dalwhinnie, but isn't easily reached from anywhere. After 0.5 mile (800m), keep ahead where another track joins from the left. The joined tracks descend to a triangle junction. Turn left, gently uphill and, after 120yds (110m), bear right on to a little-used old track. This descends to a bridge over the Dall Burn.

WHERE TO EAT AND DRINK
From the head of Loch Rannoch, the former 'Road to the Isles' runs on for 5 miles (8km) to Rannoch Station. The great moor featured briefly in the film Trainspotting (1996), perhaps to show that the countryside can be as bleak as any run-down corner of Edinburgh. The austere impression is rather spoilt by the warm and friendly little café in the listed Swiss chalet-style station building. It's open from March to October.

❹ Some 120yds (110m) after the bridge, the track bends left; here a path descends on the right. This is the Black Wood of Rannoch, now a forest reserve. The path runs under beautiful pines and birches. On the right, the Dall Burn is sometimes in sight and can always be heard. The path is quite rough, but unmistakable as it cuts through deep bilberry and heather. After a mile (1.6km), the path bends left to a track. Turn right to leave the Caledonian Reserve at a notice board. At a T-junction, turn left, away from the bridge leading into the former school. The track improves as it runs past the school's indoor swimming pool and back to the lochside road.

Blair Castle and Glen Tilt

*Following Queen Victoria into the great
through-route of the Grampians.*

DISTANCE 6.5 miles (10.4km)   **MINIMUM TIME** 3hrs 15min

ASCENT/GRADIENT 852ft (260m) ▲▲▲   **LEVEL OF DIFFICULTY** ✦✦✦

PATHS Estate tracks and smooth paths, 1 stile

LANDSCAPE Castle grounds, woodland, wild river valley and mountains

SUGGESTED MAP OS Explorers 386 Pitlochry & Loch Tummel; 394 Atholl

START/FINISH Grid reference: NN 866662 (on Explorer 386)

DOG FRIENDLINESS Keep on lead in open grazing land

PARKING Blair Castle main car park

PUBLIC TOILETS Blair Atholl Centre; Blair Castle

NOTE Track goes through firing range and is closed on a few days each year.
Consult Atholl Estate Ranger service

Since humans first arrived, Tilt has been a natural highway. Robert the Bruce marched down Glen Tilt in 1306 on his way to a minor defeat near Tyndrum. Some 200 years later James V and Mary, Queen of Scots attended a deer drive in 1529, but the next monarch to complete the whole route was Queen Victoria. She came this way with Prince Albert on the third of their 'great expeditions' from Balmoral. Along with the Christmas tree and the 'Scottish Baronial' style of architecture, multi-day hill walks were ideas introduced by the Prince Consort. Today we'd call it backpacking, except that then the packs were carried by ponies and so were the people for much of the way. Even so, 69 miles (111km) from Dalwhinnie to Balmoral in a day was a considerable trek. Two bagpipers forded the Tarff side-stream waist deep, playing all the time, while the Queen came behind on her pony, led by John Brown.

An Angry Duke

Kings and cattle thieves, soldiers and shepherds have used Glen Tilt for thousands of years, and its right-of-way status is self-evident. But in 1840, the then Duke of Atholl, whose castle lay at its foot, felt he could make his own law. He did, after all, boast Britain's only private army. He tried to turn back a botanical expedition lead by Professor Balfour. The professor won the right to walk here, and his victory is commemorated in a ballad:

> There's ne'er a kilted chiel
> Shall drive us back this day, man.
> It's justice and it's public richt
> We'll pass Glen Tilt afore the nicht,
> For Dukes shall we care ae bawbee?
> The road's as free to you and me
> As to his Grace himself, man.

GLEN TILT

Responsible Access

Today a general right of responsible access to all hill ground has been made law by the Scottish Parliament. An 'Access Code' defines responsible access. During the deer-stalking season, from mid-August to October, polite and reasonable requests from the estate will be respected by hill walkers. Such a request is made at Gilbert's Bridge (Point ❹).

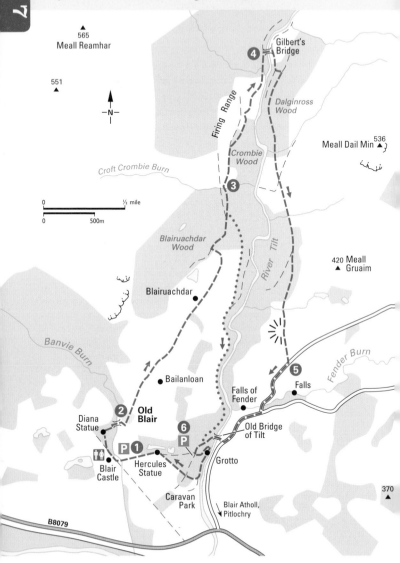

WALK 7 DIRECTIONS

❶ Turn right in front of the castle to a six-way signpost, and bear right for a gate into Diana's Grove. Bear left on a wide path to

Diana herself. Turn right on a path that leads to a giant redwood tree and then bear left, to cross Banvie Burn on a footbridge alongside a road bridge. Soon a gate leads you to the road.

GLEN TILT

2 You are now at Old Blair. Follow Minigaig Street ahead uphill. It eventually becomes a track and enters forest. Ignore a track on the left and, in another 0.25 mile (400m), fork right. In 60yds (55m) you pass a path down to the right with a green waymarker. This is the return route if the firing range ahead is closed. Otherwise keep ahead to emerge from the trees at the firing range gate.

WHERE TO EAT AND DRINK

At Blair Atholl Watermill and Tea Room they don't just bake their own scones and shortbread, the flour and oatmeal are also ground on the premises. The mill dates from 1613, but the tea room is more recent; both are open from Easter to October (dogs in outdoor seating area).

3 A red flag flies here if the range is in use, but read the notice carefully as on most firing days the track route through the range may be used. Follow the main track gently downhill, well below the firing range targets, until you get to the riverside, then fork right to reach Gilbert's Bridge.

4 Cross and turn right over a cattle grid. Follow the track for 220yds (201m), then turn left up

WHILE YOU'RE THERE

White-painted Blair Castle dominates Glen Garry. It claims to be the most-visited historic house in Scotland, with Queen Victoria, Bonnie Prince Charlie and Robert the Bruce among its early guests. Under a fine set of turrets and battlements, it has 32 elegant apartments in styles covering five centuries. Blair was one of the first of Scotland's private houses to open its doors to the public.

WHAT TO LOOK OUT FOR

After a visit to admire the nearby Falls of Bruar in 1787, Robert Burns in his Humble Petition of Bruar Water appealed to the Duke of Atholl to plant more trees. The duke took the hint, with 27 million conifers going into the estate over 50 years. Diana's Grove is named after the Roman goddess of hunting, whose statue stands among 100-year-old specimens of various exotic conifers. Recent measurements show that several are Britain's biggest of their species.

a steep little path under trees to a stile. A green track now runs down-valley with fine views. It passes along the top of a larch wood. Once through a gate into the birchwood, keep on the main track, gently uphill. After the gateway out of the wood, there's a view across Blair Castle to Schiehallion. Another gate leads to a gravel track, then a tarred road.

5 Turn right, down a long hill, crossing some waterfalls on the way down. At the foot of the hill turn right, signed 'Old Blair', to cross the Old Bridge of Tilt, then turn left into a car park.

6 Just to the right of a signboard, yellow waymarkers indicate a path that passes under trees to the River Tilt. Turn right through an exotic grotto until wooden steps on the right lead up to the corner of a caravan park. Head directly away from the river under pines. Ignore a track on the right and, at the corner of the caravan park, keep ahead under larch trees following a faint path. Cross a track to take the big beech avenue towards Blair Castle. Bear left when you reach a statue of Hercules, passing the Hercules Garden to the front of the castle.

The Braes o' Killiecrankie

A deeply wooded riverside leads from the famous battlefield to Loch Faskally.

DISTANCE	8.75 miles (14.1km)
MINIMUM TIME	4hrs
ASCENT/GRADIENT	492ft (150m) ▲▲▲
LEVEL OF DIFFICULTY	+++
PATHS	Wide riverside paths, minor road, no stiles
LANDSCAPE	Oakwoods on banks of two rivers
SUGGESTED MAP	OS Explorer 386 Pitlochry & Loch Tummel
START/FINISH	Grid reference: NN 917626
DOG FRIENDLINESS	Off lead on riverside paths
PARKING	Killiecrankie Visitor Centre
PUBLIC TOILETS	At start

Ye wouldna been sae swanky o
If ye'd hae seen where I hae seen
On the braes o' Killiecrankie o'

The song commemorating the victory of the Battle of Killiecrankie in 1689 is still sung in many a pub full of patriotic tourists, despite the fact that both sides in the battle were Scots. When James II was ousted from England in a bloodless coup in 1688, the Scots Parliament (the Estates) voted to replace him with William of Orange. The Stuarts had neglected and mismanaged Scotland, and had mounted a bloody persecution of the fundamentalist Protestants (Covenanters) of the Southern Uplands.

'Bluidy Clavers'

John Claverhouse, 'Bonnie Dundee', had earned the nickname 'Bluidy Clavers' in those persecutions. He now raised a small army of Highlanders in support of King James. The Estates sent a larger army north under another Highlander, General Hugh Mackay. Dundee, outnumbered two to one, was urged to ambush Mackay in the Pass of Killiecrankie but refused, on the grounds of chivalry. The path above the river was steep, muddy and wide enough for only two soldiers; a surprise attack on this ground would give his broadsword-wielding Highlanders too great an advantage against Mackay's inexperienced troops. Just one of the Lowlanders was picked off by an Atholl sharpshooter at the Trouper's Den (below today's visitor centre), and the battle took place on open ground, north of the pass.

Claymore Victorious

Killiecrankie was the last time the claymore conquered the musket in open battle, due to a deficiency in the musket. Some 900 of the 2,500 Highlanders were shot down as they charged, but then the troopers had to stop to fix their bayonets, which plugged into the muzzle of the musket. By this time the Highlanders were upon them, and they broke and fled. The battle lasted just three minutes. Half of Mackay's army was killed, wounded, captured

LOCH FASKALLY

or drowned in the Garry. One escaped by leaping 18ft (5.5m) across the river: the 'Soldier's Leap'. Dundee died in battle. A month later his army was defeated at Dunkeld, and 25 years later, when the Highlanders next brought their claymores south for the Stuarts, the troupers had learnt to fix a bayonet to the side of a musket where it didn't block the barrel.

WALK 8 DIRECTIONS

❶ From the back corner of the visitor centre, steps signed 'Soldier's Leap', lead down into

the wooded gorge. A footbridge crosses the waterfall of Trouper's Den. At the next junction, turn left ('Soldier's Leap'). Ten steps down, a spur path on the right

Overleaf: The Pass of Killiecrankie (Walks 8–9)

WALK

8

leads to the viewpoint above the Soldier's Leap.

2 Return to the main path, signed 'Linn of Tummel', which runs down to the River Garry below the viaduct. After 1 mile (1.6km), it reaches a footbridge.

3 Don't cross this footbridge, but continue ahead, signed 'Pitlochry', along the riverside under the tall South Garry road bridge. The path bears left to a footbridge. Cross and turn right, signed 'Pitlochry', back to the main river. The path runs around a huge river pool to a tarred lane; turn right here. The lane leaves the lochside, then passes a track on the right, blocked by a vehicle barrier. Ignore this track but shortly afterwards turn right at another signpost to Pitlochry.

WHILE YOU'RE THERE

At the Pitlochry dam that forms Loch Faskally, Scottish and Southern Energy has a small visitor centre celebrating its hydro-electric schemes. It also has a window into the salmon ladder beside the dam. From April to October (Mon–Fri, weekends and bank holidays in July and August only) you can watch the fish battle their way up towards Killiecrankie.

4 Immediately bear left along the right-hand side of Loch Dunmore, following red-top posts. Turn away from the footbridge across the loch, half right, on to a small path that becomes a dirt track. After 270yds (246m) it reaches a wider track. Turn left, with a white/yellow waymarker. After 220yds (201m), the track starts to climb and the white/yellow markers indicate a smaller path on the right which follows the lochside to a point below the A9 road bridge.

WHERE TO EAT AND DRINK

There are cafés at the start and at Lochside, Pitlochry. Pitlochry itself is the town of the tea room. One of them is Macdonald's, on the main street, which serves traditional Scottish high teas to the very hungry.

5 Cross Loch Faskally on the Clunie footbridge below the road's bridge and turn right, on a quiet road around the loch. In 1 mile (1.6km), at the top of the grass bank on the left, is the Priest Stone. After you pass the Clunie power station, you reach a car park on the left. Here a sign indicates a steep little path down to the Linn of Tummel.

6 Return to the road above for 0.5 mile (800m), to cross a suspension bridge on the right. Turn right, downstream, to pass above the Linn. A spur path back right returns to the falls at a lower level, but the main path continues along the riverside (signed 'Killiecrankie'). It bends left and goes down wooden steps to the Garry, then continues upstream and under the high road bridge. Take the side-path up on to the bridge for the view of the river, then return to follow the descending path signed 'Pitlochry via Faskally'. This runs down to the bridge, Point **3**. Return upstream to the start.

WHAT TO LOOK OUT FOR

Loch Faskally is artificial, and you'll pass the Clunie power station on the walk. Its stone arch commemorates the five people who tragically died during the construction of the Clunie Tunnel, which brings water from Loch Tummel down to Killiecrankie.

Slopes of Ben Vrackie

*High above Glen Garry for an eagle's-eye
view of Blair Castle and Pitlochry.*

See map and information panel for Walk 8

DISTANCE 9.5 miles (15.3km)	MINIMUM TIME 5hrs
ASCENT/GRADIENT 1,575ft (480m) ▲▲▲	LEVEL OF DIFFICULTY +++

WALK 9 DIRECTIONS
(Walk 8 option)

Don't cross the Clunie footbridge over Loch Faskally (Point **5**), but keep ahead under the road bridge to the Loch Faskally Boating Station. Take its access road up to the A924 and follow this main road across the railway and into Pitlochry. The first street left is Larchwood Road (Point **A**).

Sunnybank Cottage, on this corner, is where a local man, John Stewart, stabbed his cousin Donald. He stayed in the area to spy on the funeral in the belief that if he could see light under his cousin's coffin as it passed him, he would get away with the killing. It worked: he was never charged with the crime.

Turn left up Larchwood Road. It climbs with a dog-leg to left and right, then bends right beside a pool. (From here to the end, the walk follows green-man waymarkers.) Above the golf course, you turn right to a T-junction at Moulin village (Point **B**). A standing stone called the Dane Stone is in a field on the left. Turn left here, signed 'Ben-y-Vrackie', and go up the lane into a car park on the right (Point **C**).

A path leads up the Moulin Burn. Where a track crosses, turn right for a few steps, before continuing uphill keeping the stream on your left. The path joins a higher track, then turns off on the right to a footbridge. Follow the stream up to the top of the woodland, where a gate (Point **D**) leads out on to open moor.

A wide path continues up to the right of the stream, then bends right to a bench with a fine view down Glen Garry. On joining a new stream, bear left on a smaller, stony path signed 'Bealach Walk'. (The main path ahead leads, after a stiff climb, to the summit of Ben Vrackie.) After a stile with a waymark just above, the path becomes grassier. It runs directly uphill, to pass just to the right of the obvious little pass (Point **E**) just above.

Now the path becomes a clear track through the pass leading downhill. A sign points towards Killiecrankie. The track fords a stream, with a footbridge alongside. After two gates, turn left at a T-junction (Point **F**) to continue downhill. Where the track reaches a tarred road, turn right, again signed for Killiecrankie. The road passes under the new A9 to meet the older B8079 opposite the visitor centre at the start of Walk 8.

Around Kinloch Rannoch

A wander round field paths, riversides and through a craggy wood.

DISTANCE	2.25 miles (3.6km)
MINIMUM TIME	1hr
ASCENT/GRADIENT	100ft (30m) ▲▲▲
LEVEL OF DIFFICULTY	+++
PATHS	Small but well-formed paths, sometimes muddy, 2 stiles
LANDSCAPE	Oakwoods, large river, very large loch
SUGGESTED MAP	OS Explorer 386 Pitlochry & Loch Tummel
START/FINISH	Grid reference: NN 661587
DOG FRIENDLINESS	Good, but care on short stretch of B846 without pavement
PARKING	Street parking in main square of Kinloch Rannoch
PUBLIC TOILETS	At start, in Dunalastair Hotel

WALK 10 DIRECTIONS

From the north end of the bridge over the River Tummel, walk up the right-hand side of the square, past the post office. Turn right opposite a garage towards Kinloch Rannoch Primary School. Before the school, a sign, 'Riverside Path', points to the right. The tarred path has a small stream on its left. When it reaches the Tummel, it turns left to cross the stream by a footbridge.

WHILE YOU'RE THERE

The Queen's View Visitor Centre at the east end of Loch Tummel has one of the finest views in Scotland – along the loch to Schiehallion. Inside, there's an audio-visual display.

The path continues alongside the Tummel. Where it bends left into a housing estate, a small sign, 'Riverside Path', marks the smaller earth path ahead. It passes through woodland close to the river, to emerge at a roadside car park with picnic tables.

Another 80yds (73m) along the road, a high gate on the opposite side is signed 'Hillside Path'. Through the gate, turn sharp left up steps to an earth track. This climbs gently through oak and beech woods, with the main road not far below.

The cliffs of Craig Varr are just above. A glacier that came down out of Rannoch Moor dug the bed of Loch Rannoch as it hit more level ground. It also chopped off the end of this hill spur to give Craig Varr its steep southern slope. Large boulders, cracked off by frost, have rolled down into the wood, with one huge split rock right beside the track. Its mossy condition shows that the rockfall took place long ago, and in fact it was probably during the tail-end of the ice age. Smaller stones, dislodged in the same way, form scree above the wood.

The track passes through a gate with a stile alongside. In 150yds (137m) it bends uphill; fork left here on a smaller path. This

KINLOCH RANNOCH

WALK 10

(182m) above the village with sight-lines along lochs Rannoch and Tummel, but the route bears left on a path signed 'Loch Rannoch'. A ruined wall runs below on the left. On the right you pass a stone arch containing a spring of clear water that flows into a stone tank.

A kissing gate leads to the roadside near the Rannoch Hotel. Turn left, towards the village. Take care here as there is no pavement; walk round bends on the outside so you can be seen by drivers. Just before Kinloch Rannoch, the road bends left at what is called Drive Into Loch Corner. For motorists emerging from the village, a tempting straight leads to an open gateway with the chilly waters of Rannoch just below.

At the start of the pavement, opposite the Kinloch Rannoch Medical Practice, turn right. A 'Please Shut the Gate' notice indicates the correct gate, where a rough track leads towards the riverside, surrounded by yellow-flowering broom bushes. A tall concrete weir controls the water level of Loch Rannoch here.

descends to a gate and footbridge just above the road, which it joins at the entrance to Kinloch Rannoch Outdoor Centre on the edge of the village.

Continue along the road for a few steps, crossing the Allt Mor. If you wish to shorten this already short walk, the main square is just ahead, otherwise turn sharp right on a track with a hidden public footpath sign for Loch Rannoch Hotel. A board with a path map is on the left.

On the right is a small but striking waterfall. The strata of the schist are sloped at an angle of about 45 degrees, downwards to the right. The strands of the stream run down the strata, then across them forming a diamond pattern. Allt means stream, and Mor (sometimes Mhor, but pronounced Vore) means large. A small metal man once fished the pool below the waterfall; hopefully he may return.

After an abandoned wildlife garden on the left, the route passes through a gate with a kissing gate alongside, on to a stony track. In 20yds (18m), the uphill track is signed for Craig Varr. The top of the crag is a popular viewpoint, poised 600ft

The path leads downstream, through a detached gate patterned with the Saltire (St Andrew's Cross) of Scotland and under birch trees. Alongside, the wide river roils and swirls in an unnatural fashion, caused by its passage through the weir. After passing under the road bridge, turn left past the derelict public toilets to the village square.

Into the Lost Valley

*A rugged waterfall walk into the hidden hollow
where the MacDonalds hid their stolen cows.*

DISTANCE 2.75 miles (4.4km) **MINIMUM TIME** 2hrs 15min

ASCENT/GRADIENT 1,050ft (320m) ▲▲▲ **LEVEL OF DIFFICULTY** +++

PATHS Rugged and stony, stream to wade through

LANDSCAPE Crags and mountains

SUGGESTED MAP OS Explorer 384 Glen Coe & Glen Etive

START/FINISH Grid reference: NN 168569

DOG FRIENDLINESS Dogs must be reasonably fit and agile

PARKING Lower of two roadside parking places opposite Gearr Aonach
(middle one of the Three Sisters)

PUBLIC TOILETS Glencoe village

The romantically named Lost Valley is 'Coire Gabhail' in Gaelic, the 'Corrie of Booty'. Here, during the centuries leading up to the famous massacre of 1692, the MacDonalds hid their stolen cattle when the owners came storming in over the Moor of Rannoch with torch and claymore. It seems incredible that even the sure-footed black cattle of the clans could have been persuaded up the slope to Coire Gabhail. The corrie entrance is blocked by two old landslides from the face of Gearr Aonach, the middle hill of Glen Coe's Three Sisters.

Noble Profession of Cattle Thief

The economic system of Highland Scotland, until 1745, was based on the keeping and the stealing of cattle. It was an unsettled and dangerous lifestyle, and its artform was the verse of the bard who celebrated the most ingenious or violent acts of thievery and kept track of blood feuds.

The clan, gathered under its chieftain, was an organisation for protecting its own glen and for stealing from its neighbours. The MacDonalds of Glen Coe were particularly good at it. They raided right across the country, passing the fringes of the Cairngorms to steal from Aberdeenshire and Moray. In 1689, when Campbell of Glen Lyon was a guest in the house of MacIan, chief of Glen Coe, his cold blue eyes may have dwelt on a particular cooking pot. Twice in the previous ten years, MacIan had come raiding into Glen Lyon, dishonoured the women by cutting off their hair and, on the second occasion, stolen that pot from Campbell's own mother.

The Massacre

By the late 1600s, the clan and the claymore were being replaced by a legal system backed by the central government and its army. But because they were so good at cattle thieving, the MacDonalds of Glen Coe continued the practice long after everyone else had reluctantly started to move into the modern world of cash. As a result, the government decided to make an example of them.

GLEN COE

On a cold February day, a squad of soldiers arrived in the valley. Traditional hospitality meant that even its leader from Glen Lyon, a Campbell and an enemy, was welcomed into the house of MacDonald. Five nights later, at a given signal, the soldiers rose and murdered their hosts. The Glen Coe Massacre was either incompetent or mercifully half-hearted. Of the valley's population of 300, just 40 were killed, with the remainder escaping through the snow to the Lost Valley and other high corries.

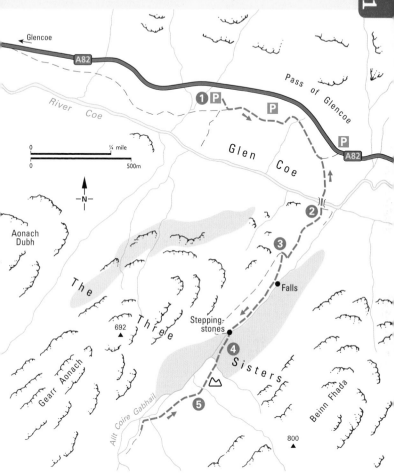

WALK 11 DIRECTIONS

1 From the uphill corner of the car park, a faint path slants down to the old road, which is now a well-used wide path. Head up the valley for about 650yds (594m). With the old road continuing as a green track ahead, your path now bends down to the right. It has been rebuilt, with the bog

problem solved by scraping down to the bedrock. The path reaches the gorge where the River Coe runs in a geological dyke of softer rock. Descend here on a steep wooden step ladder, to cross a spectacular footbridge.

2 The ascent out of the gorge is on a bare rock staircase. Above, the path runs through

41

regenerating birch wood, which can be very wet on the legs; sheep and deer have been excluded from the wood with a temporary fence. Emerge from this through a high gate. The path, rebuilt in places, runs uphill for 60yds (55m). Here it bends left; an inconspicuous alternative path continues uphill, which can be used to bypass the narrow path of the main route.

WHERE TO EAT AND DRINK

The Clachaig Inn, on the old road to Glencoe village, has been the haunt of hill people around here for over a century. It serves hearty food, several real ales and over 100 whiskies. The Boots Bar is well accustomed to tired and rather damp people coming out of the Lost Valley, though they do ask that boots be reasonably clean. Dogs are welcome, but children are only permitted in the more refined Bidean Bar.

3 The main route contours into the gorge of the Allt Coire Gabhail. It is narrow with steep drops below. Where there is an alternative of rock slabs and a narrow path just below, the slabs are more secure. You will hear waterfalls, then two fine ones come into view ahead. After passing these, continue between boulders to where the main path bends left to cross the stream below a boulder the size of a small house. (A small path runs on up to the right of the stream, but leads nowhere useful.) The river here is wide and fairly shallow. Five or six stepping-stones usually allow dry crossing. If the water is above the stones, then it's safer to wade alongside them; if the water is more than knee-deep the crossing should not be attempted.

4 A well-built path continues uphill, now with the stream on

WHILE YOU'RE THERE

The National Trust for Scotland's new visitor centre is on the A82 opposite Glencoe village. (The earlier one, below the towering face of Bidean nan Bian, was removed in 1999 as an intrusion.) The centre tells the story of the glen, the MacDonalds and the Massacre of Glen Coe.

its right. After 100yds (91m) a lump of rock blocks the way. The path follows a slanting ramp up its right-hand side. It continues uphill, still rebuilt in places, passing above the boulder pile that blocks the valley, the result of two large rockfalls from under Gearr Aonach opposite. At the top of the rockpile the path levels, giving a good view into the Lost Valley.

5 Drop gently to the valley's gravel floor. The stream vanishes into the gravel, to reappear below the boulder pile on the other side. Note where the path arrives at the gravel, as it becomes invisible at that point. Wander up the valley to where the stream vanishes, 0.25 mile (400m) ahead. Anywhere beyond this point is more serious hillwalking than you have done up to now on this walk. Return to the path and follow it back to the start of the walk.

WHAT TO LOOK OUT FOR

Aonach Dubh is the right-hand of the Three Sisters of Glen Coe. High on its flank is the black slot of Ossian's Cave. Ossian was the bard to the Fingalians, a race of legendary giants who roamed the hills before the coming of the clans. His cave is hard to get to – a rock climb graded 'Difficult' – and is most uncomfortable, as its floor slopes at an angle of 45 degrees.

Around the Small Shepherd

*Two valley passes through the high mountains
at the head of Glen Coe.*

DISTANCE *8 miles (12.9km)*	MINIMUM TIME *4hrs 30min*
ASCENT/GRADIENT *1,300ft (396m)* ▲▲▲	LEVEL OF DIFFICULTY +++

PATHS *Rough, unmade paths, some boggy bits, no stiles*

LANDSCAPE *Remote high valleys into heart of hills*

SUGGESTED MAP *OS Explorer 384 Glen Coe & Glen Etive*

START/FINISH *Grid reference: NN 213559*

DOG FRIENDLINESS *Good, some streams to cross*

PARKING *Large parking area on south side of A82, marked by yellow
AA phone post*

PUBLIC TOILETS *Glencoe village*

NOTE *Fords in Lairig Eilde can be impassible or dangerous after heavy rain*

This walk uses two through-routes on either side of Buachaille Etive Beag, the 'Small Herdsman of Etive'. The Gaelic word 'Lairig' means a valley pass through the mountains. We follow Lairig Gartain for the outward part of the journey, and Lairig Eilde for the return, with a final link along the old Glencoe road.

Passing Deer

This land is owned by the National Trust for Scotland, and there hasn't been any deer stalking for 65 years. If you are really lucky, you might hear the mountain walls echoing with the roaring of the stags as you walk through Lairig Eilde ('Pass of the Deer'). It's an unforgettable sound – rather like a lion, but a little like a cow too.

For most of the year the hinds gather in small family groups with their calves of the last two years, while the stags go around in loose gangs. Deer dislike midges, so in summer they'll be on the high tops, though they may come down at night or in bad weather. In winter they'll be in the valley bottom or even at the roadside. The calves are born in early June; they are dappled to camouflage them on the forest floor, which is their natural home. Within a few days they're running with the herd. The grace and speed of a week-old deer calf across a peat bog is the envy of any hillwalker.

The hinds have no antlers. The stags lose theirs in early summer and grow new ones ready for the rut: the September mating season. Large, many-branched antlers do not make a stag a better fighter, and are a serious drain on his system. They have probably evolved as display items, for intimidating other males and attracting females. A mighty roar may gain the stag the harem of a dozen hinds that he's after. If not, a quick clash of antlers will usually settle the matter. These displays are a way of determining which stag would have won without putting either to the risk of injury. However, the stag is sometimes prepared to fight for his wives and such fights can end in the death of one or even both males.

GLEN COE

Red deer owe their widespread survival in Scotland to the men who preserved and nurtured them in order to hunt them every autumn. For ancient aristocrats and newly rich Victorian manufacturers, the sport of sneaking up on a stag with a rifle was exciting, virile and also impressively expensive. With no predators, deer must still be culled by shooting, even on NTS land where no sport stalking takes place. Such culling will be done at dawn, before walkers start disturbing the hill.

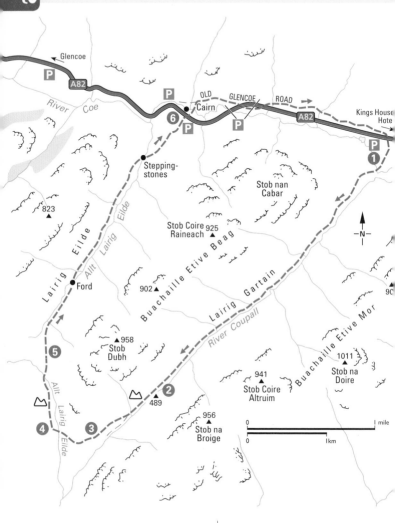

WALK 12 DIRECTIONS

❶ A signpost to Glen Etive, at the edge of the car park, marks the start of the path into Lairig Gartain. The path is clear, but very boggy in places. It heads up-valley with the River Coupall down on

the left. Gradually it draws closer to the river, but does not cross it. A large cairn marks the top of the path, which is slightly to the right of the lowest point of the pass.

❷ The descending path is steeper, first down boggy grass, then stony and eroded to the right of the stream. After 0.5 mile (800m) the main path bears off right, and slants down the right-hand wall of the valley. Eventually it emerges on to the steep south ridge of Stob Dubh.

3 Here a path runs down to a gate in a deer fence just below, but there's no need to go any further downhill. Follow a path above the deer fence, descending to cross the Allt Lairig Eilde. If the stream is too full to cross, you can return and go down through the deer fence to a wider but shallower crossing, 200yds (183m) downstream. Alternatively, you can head up on a small path to the right of the stream, hoping to find a safer crossing higher up. Having crossed the stream, follow the fence up to pass its corner. Turn right up a wide path that rises out of Glen Etive.

4 The path ascends to the left of the stream, passing several waterfalls. Eventually it crosses the stream, now very much smaller, then continues straight ahead, crossing the col well to the right of its lowest point. A large cairn marks the top of the path.

5 The new, descending stream is also, confusingly, the Allt Lairig Eilde. The path crosses it by a wide, shallow ford and goes down its left bank. A mile (1.6km) further on, the path recrosses, using large boulders as stepping-stones. It runs down to join the A82 near the cairn that marks the entry into Glen Coe.

6 Cross the road, and the river beyond, to join the old Glencoe road at an arched culvert. Turn right along the firm track, which soon rejoins the new road, then cross diagonally, on to a damp path. This runs to the right of the new road, then recrosses. It soon rejoins the A82 opposite the beginning of the walk.

Grey Mare's Tail and Mamore Lodge

*A waterfall, a shooting lodge and a ramble
down the West Highland Way.*

> **DISTANCE** *3.5 miles (5.7km)* **MINIMUM TIME** *2hrs 15min*
>
> **ASCENT/GRADIENT** *984ft (300m)* ▲▲▲ **LEVEL OF DIFFICULTY** ✦✦✦
>
> **PATHS** *Well-made paths, one steep, rough ascent, no stiles*
>
> **LANDSCAPE** *Birchwoods leading to long views along Loch Leven*
>
> **SUGGESTED MAP** *OS Explorer 384 Glen Coe & Glen Etive or
> 392 Ben Nevis & Fort William*
>
> **START/FINISH** *Grid reference: NN 187622 on OS Explorer 384*
>
> **DOG FRIENDLINESS** *Off lead unless sheep near by*
>
> **PARKING** *Grey Mare's Tail car park, Kinlochleven*
>
> **PUBLIC TOILETS** *Kinlochleven, at bridge over River Leven*

Aluminium is a very common metal: around eight per cent of the earth's crust is made up of it. But, it's very reactive, which means that it's extremely difficult to extract the aluminium atoms out of the ore called bauxite. There is no chemical method for this process. Instead, it's done by dissolving the ore in molten cryolite (a fluoride mineral) and applying vast quantities of electricity. As a result, aluminium processing doesn't take place where you find the bauxite, but where you find the electricity, with lots of water coming down steep hillsides, and a deep-water harbour at the bottom, such as Kinlochleven.

The village of Kinlochleven was built around the smelter. Two lochs above have been dammed for hydro-electricity, and six huge pipes bring the water down from a control station above the Devil's Staircase footpath.

Pipeline or Path

A pipeline on the OS Landranger map is a dotted line, rather like a path. And it may be that the path of this walk happened by mistake, as walkers mistook the pipeline for a path, walked along it and so created the path that they thought was there in the first place.

The pipeline path leads from the outflow of Loch Eilde Mor, around the head of Loch Leven along the 1,100ft (335m) contour, giving superb views towards the Pap of Glencoe and the loch's foot. Eventually, it carries Loch Eilde's water to the Blackwater Reservoir.

Why has the water from Loch Eilde been taken all the way round this hillside to the Blackwater Reservoir, instead of straight down to the turbines where it's actually needed? You need to glance across the valley at the six descending pipes for the answer. At the foot of those huge reinforced pipes the water is under 30 tons per square foot (300 tonnes/sq m) of pressure. A second such set from Loch Eilde would cost far more than the much longer, unpressurised pipe to the other reservoir.

The Kinlochmore smelter started as one of the largest in the world, but by the end of the 1900s it was the world's smallest. It closed in 2000,

KINLOCHLEVEN

although its turbines continue to generate electricity, which is now diverted to the smelter at Fort William or into the National Grid. The smelter had been the reason for Kinlochleven, and its main employer. Projects to keep Kinlochleven alive include the fine, newly constructed path system, the visitor centre and the Atlas Brewery on the site where carbon electrical connectors were once made.

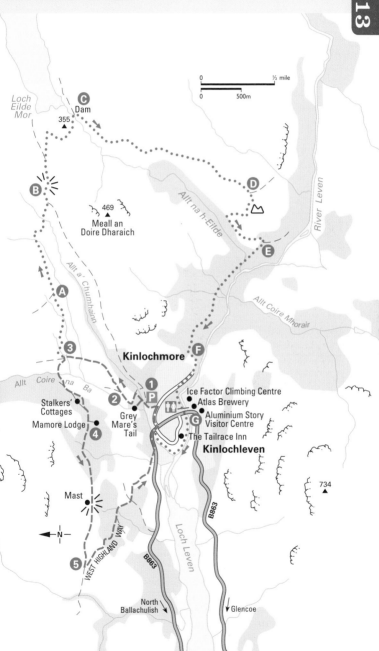

KINLOCHLEVEN

WALK 13 DIRECTIONS

WALK 13 *(margin)*

1 A smooth gravel path leads up out of the car park to multicoloured waymarkers pointing left. The path rises to a view through trees of the Grey Mare's Tail waterfall, then descends to a footbridge. Here turn left (blue waymarker) to visit the foot of the spectacular waterfall, then return to take the path on the right (white, yellow and green waymarker). Follow the stream up for 100yds (91m), then turn left at a waymarker. The path, quite steep and loose, zig-zags up through birches to reach more open ground.

WHILE YOU'RE THERE

The Aluminium Story Visitor Centre at Kinlochleven is worth a quick visit, housed in the local library. Alternatively, you could tour the Atlas Brewery, in a disused part of the aluminium works (Mon–Sat, 5:30pm).

2 Here the path forks. Take the right-hand branch, with a yellow and green waymarker, to pass under power lines. The path runs through scattered birch to a gate in a deer fence, then bends left to cross over two streams. Immediately after the second stream is another junction.

3 The confusing waymarker here has eight arrows in four colours. Turn left, following a white arrow slightly downhill, to cross a footbridge above a waterfall and red granite rocks. The path leads up under birches. Here the ground cover includes the aromatic bog myrtle, which can be used to discourage midges. When the path reaches a track, turn left. Below the track is a tin deer used by stalkers for target practice: it's more convenient than

WHERE TO EAT AND DRINK

The Tailrace Inn, in Kinlochleven, is a service station on the West Highland Way. They welcome children (if having a meal) and dogs (if well behaved). In summer, you won't get through an evening without a rousing chorus of Bonnie Banks of Loch Lomond. Try the Atlas Brewery's 'Wayfarer' ale, brewed for thirsty West Highland Way walkers.

the real thing as it doesn't wander off just when you're creeping up on it. A signed footpath bypasses the Stalkers' Cottages on the left, then rejoins the track beyond, to a junction above Mamore Lodge.

4 Keep ahead, above the lodge, climbing gently past two tin huts, self-catering accommodation labelled 'stable' and 'bothy'. At the high point of the track there is a TV mast on the right, a bench on the left and a view along Loch Leven ahead. The track descends gently, with slabs of whitish quartzite above. The wide path of the West Highland Way (WHW) can be seen below and gradually rises to join the track, with a large waymarker planted in a cairn.

5 Turn left down the West Highland Way path, which drops into the woods below. Watch out for a junction where the main path seems to double back to the right; take the smaller path, continuing ahead with a WHW waymarker. After crossing the tarred access track of Mamore Lodge, the path fords a small stream to reach the village. Turn left along the pavement and fork left into Wades Road to regain the car park.

Aluminium Landscape Above Kinlochleven

A sea loch, a mountain loch and a pipeline path above deep wooded glens.
See map and information panel for Walk 13

DISTANCE 6.75 *miles* (10.9km)	MINIMUM TIME *3hrs 45min*
ASCENT/GRADIENT *1,400ft (427m)* ▲▲▲	LEVEL OF DIFFICULTY ✚✚✚

WALK 14 DIRECTIONS (Walk 13 option)

Follow Walk 13 up to Point **3**. At this junction turn right, following a yellow waymarker. The path climbs beside a stream, then bends right to cross it. It passes through a deer fence gate to reach a track (Point **A**). A continuation path rises briefly past a stone bench on an outcrop of red-orange rhyolite, then rejoins the track.

Follow the track uphill towards a wide pass. Just before it, a path on the right is a short-cut back to Kinlochleven. At the pass (Point **B**) is a view ahead along Loch Eilde Mor, which translates from Gaelic as Big Loch of the Hind.

Descend for 0.25 mile (400m) to a path forking off on the right. After 330yds (300m), bend right. A smaller path ahead goes only to the loch foot, while the main path leads to the right of a knoll to a dam over the Allt na h-Eilde (Point **C**).

Turn right on to a rough and soggy track. This follows a concrete pipeline across the hill face, high above Kinlochleven, with fine views. In the pipeline below, look out for a rusty metal item like a tea-strainer on a stick – this is a pressure release valve. After 1.25 miles (2km), the path drops below the pipeline and, in another 200yds (183m), a cairn marks a steep path descending on the right (Point **D**).

To the left you should see the Crowberry Tower on distant Buachaille Etive Mor, outlined against the sky. The path zig-zags downhill until it enters the wood, but then rises slightly to join another path (Point **E**). Turn right on this path. When you see buildings ahead, the main path forks down left to the edge of Kinlochleven (Point **F**).

The track ahead has a West Highland Way marker. Shortly it becomes a street; look for the tarred path on the left where the WHW turns back to the riverside. You pass the tailrace at the former smelter and continue to the road bridge (Point **G**). You can turn up right into Kinlochleven here. For a longer walk, continue under the bridge to a riverside path. It bends right, past black garages, to an earth path upstream alongside the Allt Coire na Ba. Where the path ends, a few steps ahead, you cross the B863 into Wade Road. This leads to the car park.

Waterfalls and Wade's Walk

A sheltered forest ramble high above Loch Linnhe.

DISTANCE 2.75 miles (4.4km)	**MINIMUM TIME** 1hr 30min
ASCENT/GRADIENT 600ft (183m) ▲▲▲	**LEVEL OF DIFFICULTY** +++

PATHS Well-made paths, forest tracks, no stiles

LANDSCAPE Plantation and semi-wild forest

SUGGESTED MAP OS Explorer 384 Glen Coe & Glen Etive

START/FINISH Grid reference: NN 029634

DOG FRIENDLINESS Off lead in forest

PARKING Forest Enterprise picnic place at road end, behind Inchree

PUBLIC TOILETS Corran Ferry – bypass ferry queue and turn left into car park

NOTE Timber felling over the next few years may affect parts of the route, but the first stage to the waterfalls should remain accessible throughout. Contact Lochaber Forest District on 01397 702184 for details

WALK 15 DIRECTIONS

At the bottom corner of the car park is a well-built path marked by a blue (An Drochaid) waymarker. A field on its right gives views out across Loch Linnhe. The path then crosses a footbridge to enter woodland before running gently uphill, through birchwoods with clearings of heather and grass. The Inchree waterfalls appear ahead, falling through a steep gorge lined with rhododendron.

There are seven waterfalls, though only the top three are visible from here. They are particularly fine after heavy rain. The path turns uphill, staying about 100yds (91m) from the falls, but with fine views of them, particularly from two viewpoint spurs on the right. Where the path is carved into the hillside it shows the underlying lumpy white quartzite, the same rock that gives a whitish appearance to the tops of the hills above Glen Nevis.

Above the second viewpoint, the path bends left. Here a small path runs ahead through boggy ground. This is aiming for the top of the upper fall, but it isn't recommended as the rocks alongside the fall are unsafe (wet quartzite is slippery) and you don't actually get a better view of the water.

Not far above, the path runs up to a forest road. Turn left along this. At a junction, the downward path, with red-and-white waymarkers, is a short-cut back to the car park. Your route turns uphill to the right, with a red waymarker.

WHILE YOU'RE THERE

The West Highland Museum in Fort William, is old-fashioned, with interesting items in display cases rather than screens and storyboards. There is a lock of Bonnie Prince Charlie's hair, as well as a secret picture of him that has to be viewed via a polished metal cylinder.

INCHREE

The wide path runs up under gloomy larches, with clearings formed by windblow. In economic terms it makes sense to keep planting, even where there is a slight risk of losing trees in this way. Unusually stormy winters since 1999 have made trees more vulnerable than the planters of 30 years ago, before global warming, could have expected.

A stream runs up beside the track, which bends left to cross it. As it reaches more open ground above, it is running along the line of one of General Wade's military roads (see Walk 22). This one ran from Corran Ferry to Corrychurrachan and Fort William. There's really only one way to build a basic road without tarmac. The new path illustrates the Wade technique of jammed stones, covered with finer gravel, and shows it particularly clearly as here the jammed stones are whitish quartzite while the overlying gravel is reddish granite.

The path joins the end of a forest road, with a quarry on the left. Bear left on a crossing track and, in 100yds (91m), keep ahead as another forest track runs in from the right. Red waymarkers indicate the correct track. The wide, smooth road heads downhill, with views across Loch Linnhe. A ravine on the left has been left to regenerate with a mixture of wild species and plantation escapees. The Sitka spruce is not native to Scotland, but the effect is pleasingly wild.

The slope above the forest road was clear-felled in 2002. A skyline cable was used to bring felled trees down the steep slope. This strong wire cable mounted on a standing tree trunk has to be high enough to keep the felled tree's butt above the ground on the way down, but not so high that the leverage pulls the standing tree down. The felled tree is hauled downhill by an operator in a tractor on the forest road. If the haul-in cable should break, the suddenly released end is very dangerous, and so the tractor cab is armoured for protection. If the haul-back cable breaks, the felled tree starts coming very fast, and the operator has to drop the sky line very quickly.

On a very steep slope like this one, the actual felling is the most skilled and demanding part of the job. Chainsaw operations are kept to a minimum – the trees are simply dropped to await the winch operation. Drop them wrong and they tangle up together, making the winch operation impossible. After clear-felling, replanting will be less purely commercial than last time around. The grey-green blocks of spruce will be broken up with larch.

The forest road bends to the right, with a bench that, until the branches grow in, will give a distant view of Inchree waterfalls. Turn down left on a steep path, which soon levels out to a footbridge. On reaching buildings, keep straight ahead under a narrow tree-belt to the car park.

Ariundle Oakwoods and the Elements of Chemistry

*Through the shades of green Sunart
to the hillside site of an old lead mine.*

DISTANCE 7 miles (11.3km) **MINIMUM TIME** 3hrs 45min

ASCENT/GRADIENT 950ft (290m) ▲▲▲ **LEVEL OF DIFFICULTY** +++

PATHS *Good through woodland, sketchy on open hill, no stiles*

LANDSCAPE *Ancient oakwood, open and remote hill ground*

SUGGESTED MAP *OS Explorer 391 Ardgour & Strontian*

START/FINISH *Grid reference: NM 826633*

DOG FRIENDLINESS *Keep on lead in reserve*

PARKING *Nature Reserve car park at Ariundle*

PUBLIC TOILETS *Tourist Information Centre, Strontian*

What does Strontian have in common with the hamlet of Ytterby in Sweden, with Paris (or *Lutetia* as the ancient city was called in Latin) and Copenhagen (*Hafnia* in its latinised form), with the planet Uranus and the Sun (personified as the god *Helios* in Greek mythology)? Chemical elements – the fundamental materials of nature. Seventeen of them are named after places, including ytterbium, lutetium, hafnium, uranium, helium – and strontium.

Davy the Namer

A new mineral was discovered in the lead ores of Strontian in 1793, and named strontites. Sir Humphrey Davy visited the mines in 1808 and isolated the new element strontium. Davy is remembered as the inventor of the safety lamp for miners, but he also identified and named the elements calcium, magnesium and chlorine. Strontium (Sr) comes in at number 38 in the list of chemical elements. When heated, its salts burn with a crimson flame, and it is used in making fireworks. The radioactive form strontium 90 does not occur in nature at Strontian or anywhere else, but is produced in nuclear explosions, including the Chernobyl reactor disaster. Because of its chemical similarity to calcium, strontium 90 is absorbed into the bones, where its radioactive breakdown damages the bone marrow.

The Older New York

The lead mines around Strontian, including the Bellsgrove mine reached on this walk, opened in the early 18th century. The villages around them came to be known as New York, after the York Building Company that built them. Some 60 tons of Strontian lead – one tenth of the year's output – went in 1753 to roof the new castle at Inveraray (see Walk 3). As the more accessible veins were worked out, these remote mines became uneconomic and eventually closed in 1871. They have been reopened in a small way for the extraction of the mineral barytes. The element barium, a chemical relative of calcium and strontium, is used in drilling muds for the oil industry.

STRONTIAN

On its way to the lead mine and the waterfalls of Strontian Glen, the walk passes through the Ariundle National Nature Reserve. In the mountains, the native wild wood of Scotland was the Scots pine (see Walk 6). Here on the warm, damp sea coast, the wild wood is of oak. The Ariundle oakwood owes its survival to human interference. The livestock and deer that destroyed Scotland's forest were kept out so that the oaks could be coppiced – harvested on a seven-year cycle. The timber went to the iron smelters of Bonawe on Loch Etive and the bark to the tanners. The wild oakwood is being repaired, with the felling out of commercial spruce. Beneath the dense canopy of leaves, it is carpeted in soft, glossy moss and is rich in ferns and primitive plants called liverworts. While we expect the natural world to be green, it's not often quite so green as Ariundle.

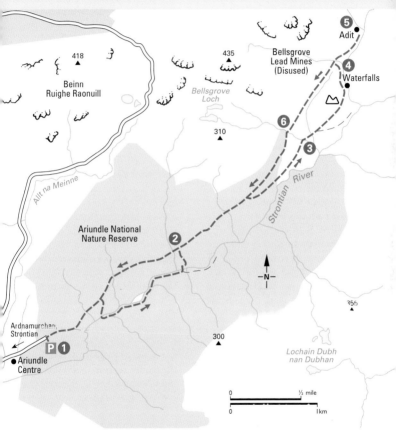

WALK 16 DIRECTIONS

❶ From the car park, continue along the track into oakwoods. After 0.25 mile (400m), ignore a pony path on the right. In another 0.25 mile (400m) a footpath turns off right. It crosses the Strontian River and heads upstream along

it. After a pleasant 0.75 mile (1.2km) it recrosses the river, following a duckboard section to rejoin the oakwood track.

❷ Turn right, away from the car park, to reach a high gate in a deer fence. The track immediately forks. Take the downward branch on the right to emerge into open grazings at river level. The track passes through a high gate and ends at a gateway and stream.

❸ Ford the stream on to a rough path. This crosses two more small streams, then forks (small cairn). The lower, right-hand branch continues alongside the Strontian River, but take the left-hand one, which is quite faint. It slants up to the left to a solitary holly tree. Here it turns straight uphill for 50yds (46m), then bends right to slant up as before, passing 200yds (183m) below a bare rock knoll. The remains of wooden steps are in the path and a few cairns stand beside it. It steepens slightly to pass below a small crag with three different trees growing out of it – rowan, hazel and oak. With a large stream and waterfalls ahead, the path turns uphill to the brink of the small gorge. Above the waterfalls, the slope eases. Just above, the path reaches the broken dam wall of a former reservoir.

❹ A green path runs across the slope just above. You can turn right on this, heading up beside the stream for about 0.25 mile

(400m). Here you will find a spoil heap; a heather bank marks the entrance to an adit – a mine tunnel running into the hill.

❺ Return along the green path past Point ❹, with the remains of the Bellsgrove Lead Mines above and below. The path improves into a track, following a stream down a small and slantwise side valley. As this stream turns down to the left, the track contours forward, to cross a wooded stream valley by a high footbridge above a waterfall.

❻ A wide, smooth track continues ahead through a gate. After 0.5 mile (800m) it rejoins the outward route at the edge of the nature reserve. Follow the track back to eventually reach the car park at Ariundle.

The Nevis Gorge and its Waterfalls

A walk beside Scotland's Himalayan lookalike,
leading to an enormous waterfall.

DISTANCE 2.5 miles (4km)   **MINIMUM TIME** 1hr 30min

ASCENT/GRADIENT 270ft (82m) ▲▲▲   **LEVEL OF DIFFICULTY** +++

PATHS Well-built path with drops alongside, no stiles

LANDSCAPE Deep wooded gorge, wet meadow above

SUGGESTED MAP OS Explorer 392 Ben Nevis & Fort William

START/FINISH Grid reference: NN 168691

DOG FRIENDLINESS Off lead, beware of steep slopes alongside path

PARKING Walkers' car park at end of Glen Nevis road

PUBLIC TOILETS Glen Nevis Visitor Centre

The Nevis Gorge, it's been said, is where Scotland pays its little tribute to the Himalayas. High walls of crag and boulder rise on either side. The path runs through a narrow gap where forest clings to the steep hillside and the river crashes below among its boulders.

Rocks and Falls Galore

Four different types of rock make up this scenery, and three of them are obvious from the walk. The crushed and ancient rocks of the Central Highlands (the Dalradian series) are mostly grey schist, but here there is also the pale-grey quartzite of Sgurr a'Mhaim, above the bend of the glen. The grinding of the continents at the time the Caledonian mountains were formed caused great bubbles of melted rock within the schist. These now appear at the surface as the granite on the lower slopes of Ben Nevis. It's grey on the outside, but pink when freshly broken or washed by streams. The granite was formed deep underground, but above it volcanoes were pouring out the black lava that now forms the summit of Ben Nevis and its formidable northern crags.

As the glen bends east towards the gorge, stop at the Polldubh car park (Grid ref: NN 145683). The first waterfall is hidden underneath the road bridge. The riverbed is the pinkish Nevis granite, cut by two dykes – vertical intrusions of volcanic rock – which the river has eroded into twin channels. Continue up the road to its end at the second car park, where the walk starts. Glen Nevis has the rounded outline of a glacial valley.

Glacier-smoothed rock below the car park has become an informal 'symbolic cemetery', commemorating those killed by the mountains they loved. Once above the gorge, the depth of the former glacier is shown by the rocks of Meall Cumhann, on the Ben Nevis (north) side. These are obviously smoothed by the ice that has passed right over the top of them.

Steall Fall

Steall Fall is about 300ft (91m) high. In a good winter it freezes completely and climbers ascend it in spiked crampons with an ice axe in each hand.

NEVIS GORGE

The valley above the fall, the Allt Coire a'Mhail, once flowed gently out into a higher version of Glen Nevis. From above, it still appears to unwary walkers to do so. Ice deepened Glen Nevis by 750ft (229m). In the following 10,000 years, the side-stream has barely started its task of eroding the hanging valley down to the level of its new endpoint.

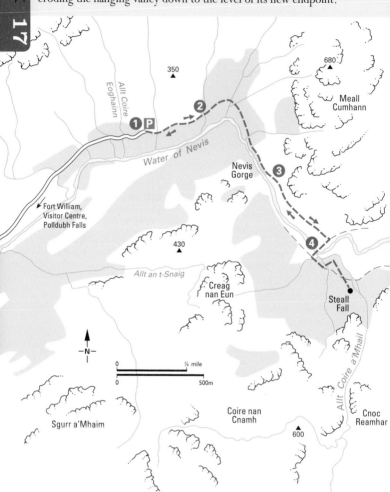

WALK 17 DIRECTIONS

1 It should be noted that the waterslide above the car park is the Allt Coire Eoghainn – if you mistake it for the Steall Fall and set off towards it you are on a difficult and potentially dangerous path. The path you will take on this walk is much easier, but even here there have been casualties, mostly caused by people wearing unsuitable shoes. At the top end of the car park you will see a signpost that shows no destination closer than the 13 miles (21km) to Kinlochleven – accordingly, this walk will be a short out-and-back. The well-made path runs gently uphill under woods of birch and hazel, across what turns into a very steep slope. For a few steps it becomes a rock-cut ledge, with a step across a waterfall side-stream.

NEVIS GORGE

WHERE TO EAT AND DRINK
The Grog & Gruel in Fort William High Street is the 'urban outpost' of Glencoe's Clahaig Inn and serves the same hearty food, with regular live music.

The path at this point is on clean pink granite, but you will see a boulder of grey schist beside the path just afterwards. Ahead, the top of the Steall Fall can now be just glimpsed through the notch of the valley.

❷ The path continues downhill to cross a stream with big rock blocks; the rock now is schist, with fine zig-zag stripes of grey and white. A short rock staircase leads to a wooden balcony section. From here the path is just above the bed of the Nevis Gorge. Here the river runs through some huge boulders, some of which bridge it completely.

❸ Quite suddenly, the path emerges on to a level meadow above the gorge. Ahead, the Steall Fall fills the view. The well-built path runs along the left-hand edge of the meadow to a point opposite the waterfall.

❹ The walk ends here, beside a footbridge which consists simply of three steel cables over a very deep pool. Those who wish to attempt the crossing should note that it gets wobblier in the middle; it's hard to turn round, but the return journey is rather easier.

From the wire bridge, the driest path runs alongside the main river round one bend before heading up to the foot of the waterfall. The view from directly beneath is even more spectacular.

The Glen Nevis Visitor Centre (Ionad Nibheis) has a detailed account of the geology and glacial effects that you will see in Glen Nevis and audio-visual displays on the natural history of the area. It also sells postcards and snacks. There are picnic tables where you can watch the walkers coming down from Ben Nevis and wonder which ones got to the top.

WHAT TO LOOK OUT FOR
At Point 2, where the path dips to cross a stream, hot rocks have penetrated cracks in the grey schist to form intrusive dykes. Two different ones are visible in the bare rock underfoot. The granite has squeezed into the older schist to form a vein of pink porphyry. Near by, superheated steam has lifted the minerals out of the schist itself and these have recondensed to a vein of whitish quartz. These intrusions are much clearer to see when the rock is wet (which it usually is).

Overleaf: Across Loch Linnhe lies Fort William, sheltered by Ben Nevis (Walk 18)

Half Ben Nevis

*The half-way lochan and the great
north corrie of Nevis.*

DISTANCE 10 miles (16.1km)	**MINIMUM TIME** 6hrs 15min
ASCENT/GRADIENT 2,000ft (610m) ▲▲▲	**LEVEL OF DIFFICULTY** +++

PATHS Hill paths, well-built, then very rough, 4 stiles

LANDSCAPE Slopes of Britain's biggest hill

SUGGESTED MAP OS Explorer 392 Ben Nevis & Fort William

START/FINISH Grid reference: NN 123731

DOG FRIENDLINESS Keep on lead through Achintee grazings, by River Nevis

PARKING Large car park at Glen Nevis Visitor Centre

PUBLIC TOILETS At start

For 21 years in the 19th century, an observatory was sited on the summit of Ben Nevis. It recorded, to the surprise of few, that this is one of the wettest spots in Britain. Averaged over the year, the summit is sunny for about two hours per day.

This walk of half the hill shows you the mountain's great northern crags and the rocky hollow of Coire Leis. The further edge of the corrie is the jagged line of Tower Ridge, Britain's longest rock climb. In early spring the damp Atlantic winds coat the crags in thick hoar-frost, over which climbers with crampons and ice axes have created hundreds of routes.

Charles Wilson, a grammar school teacher turned Cambridge professor, came to Ben Nevis on holiday in 1894. The Scottish-born professor was so struck by the effects of sunlight on the clouds above Coire Leis that he attempted to reproduce them in the Cavendish Laboratory. In so doing he invented the Wilson cloud chamber, for which he was awarded the Nobel Prize for Physics in 1927.

In summer, the moist Atlantic air that sweeps into Coire Leis condenses into cloud, and then rain. Each droplet forms around a 'nucleation centre' such as a speck of dust. Perfectly clean air can become supersaturated: it has more than enough moisture to form clouds, but can't. When moist air rises up Ben Nevis it expands due to the drop in pressure. As it expands it cools, allowing the water droplets to appear. In Wilson's cloud chamber, the pressure drop was achieved with a bicycle pump working backwards. One pull of the pump handle, and any passing particle became suddenly visible as a pencil-line of white cloud. The step-up in size is astonishing: it's as if a model aeroplane left a vapour trail as wide as the solar system, visible to an observer on another star! High energy particles can be seen zipping through the cloud chamber. Thus the positron (the positive electron) was discovered in 1932 and the muon (an exotic heavy electron) in 1937. It is actually possible to make your own Wilson cloud chamber – simply cool air with dry ice and shine a torch in. The successor to the cloud chamber was devised while gazing into a glass of beer. Donald Glaser earned the Nobel Prize for his bubble chamber in 1960.

WALK 18 DIRECTIONS

1 At the downstream corner of the car park, a bridge crosses the River Nevis. The path turns upstream, then crosses fields to a track. Cross on to the signed 'Ben Path' to Ben Nevis. After a long climb, a notice points you to a zig-zag up left on to the half-way plateau. The path passes above Lochan Meall an t-Suidhe, the Halfway Lochan, down on the left.

2 The main path takes a sharp turn back to the right, heading for the summit. Your path descends ahead, behind a wall-like cairn. After 0.25 mile (400m), bear right on a very rough path that climbs gently over peat bog to a cairn on the skyline. Here it becomes rough and rocky as it slants down across the steep slide slope of the valley of Allt a'Mhuilinn. Eventually it joins the stream and runs up beside it to the Charles Inglis Clark (CIC) Hut.

3 Return for 100yds (91m) and cross the stream on the right to join a clear path which leads downhill. This descends a rocky step with a waterslide and reaches a ladder stile into plantations.

4 Go down a forest road, which bends left across a bridge, then contours across open hill. After 0.5 mile (800m) the main track turns downhill in zig-zags. At the slope foot, it passes under power

lines. In another 220yds (201m), take a smaller track on the right, signed 'Distillery', soon to rejoin the Allt a'Mhuilinn. Pass out between distillery buildings to reach the A82.

5 Cross the River Lochy on Victoria Bridge opposite and turn left into a fenced-off side road and left again along a street. It rises to a railway bridge. Turn left here on the long Soldiers Bridge back across the Lochy. At its end, turn right over a stile for a riverside path. This soon joins the hard surfaced Great Glen Way path. This becomes a built path into woodland. After two footbridges, bear left on a smaller path to the edge of Inverlochy. Turn right, then left into a street with copper beeches. This leads through Montrose Square to the A82.

6 The street opposite is signed 'Ben Nevis Footpath'. Shortly, take a stone bridge to the Glen Nevis road. Turn left for 0.25 mile (400m) to a track on the left. Recross the Nevis on a green footbridge and turn right to a small riverside footpath. This rejoins the road briefly, then leads up-river to the footbridge at Glen Nevis Visitor Centre.

The Peat Road to Cow Hill

Another loop looking down at Fort William and up at Ben Nevis.
See map and information panel for Walk 18

DISTANCE 7.25 miles (11.7km)	MINIMUM TIME 3hrs 30min
ASCENT/GRADIENT 1,000ft (305m) ▲▲▲	LEVEL OF DIFFICULTY +++

WALK 19 DIRECTIONS
(Walk 18 option)

The following directions from the Glen Nevis Visitor Centre are the end of Walk 18 in reverse. If you are doing Walk 18 as well, you can start this loop just after Point ⑥ by turning right to the Old Fort and then picking up these directions from there.

From the Glen Nevis Visitor Centre (Point ① and the end of Walk 18), follow the riverbank to a footbridge signed 'Ben Nevis Path'. Cross and follow a small path to the left, downstream. With the road just ahead, a riverside path forks off to the left. The path and road rejoin after 0.5 mile (800m) and lead down to a green metal footbridge (Point Ⓐ).

Cross and turn right, down the Glen Nevis road to a roundabout and go left into Fort William. Bear right past the entrance to the station. Here an underpass on the left leads into the main street, but the walk bears right, in front of the Morrisons supermarket to a roundabout. Beyond is the old fort (Point Ⓑ), now the start point for the new Great Glen Way. The pavement alongside the loch leads to a car park.

From the far corner of the car park (Point Ⓒ), cross the A82 and go up to the right of a school to join a tarred path under trees. This leads up to Lundavra Road. Turn uphill to the top of the town and across a cattle grid with a kissing gate alongside to a gate on the left signed 'Keep Clear 24hr Access' (Point Ⓓ). This is the Peat Road, formed by sledges bringing peat for fuel off the hill. It rises over the moor to bend left past a path on the right signed for Glen Nevis (Point Ⓔ). But for now, continue ahead along the smooth track to the summit of Cow Hill, with views down on to Fort William and along Lochs Linnhe and Eil.

Return down the track to the side path for Glen Nevis (Point Ⓔ). Follow this well-made path into woodland. Ignore a multi-user trail left, and later a boardwalk path right; the main path descends steeply to reach a forest road. Go straight across to a continuing path with the thistle waymarker of the West Highland Way. At the valley floor, an old burial ground, with atmospheric beeches and table tombs of the early 19th century, is up on the left (Point Ⓕ) – a gate and footbridge give access to it. The main path soon leads to the Glen Nevis road.

Turn left along the pavement for 130yds (118m) and cross to a footpath under trees to return to the visitor centre.

Banks of the Caledonian Canal

A walk alongside — and underneath — Thomas Telford's masterpiece of civil engineering.

DISTANCE 4.5 miles (7.2km)	MINIMUM TIME 1hr 45min
ASCENT/GRADIENT 100ft (30m) ▲▲▲	LEVEL OF DIFFICULTY ✦✦✦

PATHS Wide tow paths, no stiles

LANDSCAPE Banks of wide canal, shore of tidal loch

SUGGESTED MAP OS Explorer 392 Ben Nevis & Fort William

START/FINISH Grid reference: NN 097768

DOG FRIENDLINESS Sensible dogs off lead on tow path

PARKING Kilmallie Hall, Corpach

PUBLIC TOILETS None en route

WALK 20 DIRECTIONS

Scotland's great coast-to-coast canal, opened in 1822, is just one of the masterpieces of civil engineering by Thomas Telford. The poet laureate, Robert Southey (1774–1843) referred to Telford as 'Pontifex Maximus', the Biggest Bridge-builder. As well as the old-style stone bridge, Telford became the master of two entirely new techniques — the cast-iron arch and the first suspension bridges. While working on the canal, he was also building 600 miles (965km) of new roads, as well as enlarging most of Scotland's harbours.

Go down past Corpach Station to the canal and cross the sea lock that separates salt water from fresh water. Follow the canal (on your left) up past another lock, where a path on the right has a blue cycle path sign and a Great Glen Way marker. It passes under tall sycamores to the shore. Follow the shoreline path past a football pitch and then turn left, across damp grass to the end of a back street. A path ahead leads up a wooded bank to the tow path.

Work on the canal started in 1803 during the Napoleonic war, and each of its 29 locks is designed to take a 40-gun frigate of Nelson's navy. Roughly 20 million wheelbarrow loads of earth were shifted over the next 19 years.

Turn right along the tow path, for 0.5 mile (800m). Just before the Banavie swing bridge, a path down to the right has a Great Glen Way marker. Follow waymarkers on street signs to a level crossing, then turn left towards the other swing bridge, the one with the road on it.

WHILE YOU'RE THERE

Much to Telford's distress, the canal was a loss-making enterprise from the day it opened. One reason was the coming of the railways. At Banavie, the West Highland Railway is Britain's most beautiful. During the summer, the steam-powered Jacobite Steam Train runs daily to Mallaig and back.

CORPACH

Just before the bridge, turn right at signs for the Great Glen Way and the Great Glen Cycle Route and continue along the tow path to Neptune's Staircase. The fanciful name was given to the locks by Telford himself. The 60ft (18m) of ascent alongside the eight locks is the serious uphill part of this walk, but more serious for boats of course. It takes about 90 minutes to work through the system. As each lock fills, slow roiling currents come up from underneath, like bath water emptying but in reverse, and as each empties, water forced under pressure into the banks emerges from the masonry in little fountains.

A gate ends the basin above the locks. About 200yds (183m) later, a grey gate on the right leads to a dump for dead cars; ignore this one. Just 220yds (201m) later the canal crosses a little wooded valley, with a black fence on the right. Now comes a second grey gate. Go through, to a track turning back sharp right and descending to ford a small stream.

On the right, the stream passes right under the canal in an arched tunnel, and alongside is a second tunnel which provides a walkers' way to the other side. Water from the canal drips into the tunnel, which has a fairly spooky atmosphere – try not to think of the large boats sailing directly over your head! At the tunnel's end, a track runs up to join the canal's northern tow path. Turn right, back down the tow path. After passing Neptune's Staircase, cross the A830 to a level crossing without warning lights. Continue along the right-hand tow path. After a mile (1.6km) the tow path track leads back to the Corpach double lock.

WHAT TO LOOK OUT FOR

From Fort William, Britain's biggest hill appears as a mere hump. The canalside, however, gives the best view into the great Northern Corrie of Ben Nevis. On its right-hand side, ranged one behind the other, rise the buttresses of the country's largest crag. Across the back runs a narrow edge of granite, linking it to the neighbouring Carn Mor Dearg. This arête is the mountaineers' preferred route to the big Ben.

WHERE TO EAT AND DRINK

The Moorings Inn at Banavie offers restaurant and bar meals to canal users and visitors. On the other side of both the A830 and canal, the unassuming Lochy family pub has picnic tables and promises 'massive portions'. At the walk start, a Keystore shop on the main road sells hot pies and the Kilmallie Hall has a community garden with picnic tables to eat them at.

A Happy Birch-day in Coire Ardair

Regenerating woodlands lead to a high pass where Bonnie Prince Charlie escaped through the window.

DISTANCE 8 miles (12.9km)	**MINIMUM TIME** 4hrs 15min
ASCENT/GRADIENT 1,400ft (427m) ▲▲▲	**LEVEL OF DIFFICULTY** +++

PATHS Very good, rough around the loch, no stiles

LANDSCAPE One-ended valley leading to lochan under crags

SUGGESTED MAP OS Explorer 401 Loch Laggan & Creag Meagaidh

START/FINISH Grid reference: NN 483872

DOG FRIENDLINESS No dogs allowed as they disturb wildlife

PARKING Nature reserve car park at Aberarder track end beside Loch Laggan

PUBLIC TOILETS None en route or near by

As the path curves westward after Point ❷, you'll see the crags of Creag Meagaidh ahead of you. When well iced up, these create many famous winter climbs. On the right, they're bounded by a narrow pass high on the skyline.

Bonnie Prince Charlie

After the defeat of the Jacobite cause at Culloden Moor on 16 April, 1746, Prince Charles Edward Stuart went on the run in the Scottish Highlands. From then until 18 September he sheltered in caves and bothies (shepherds' huts) and in the open heather. He was often hungry, usually wet, hunted by redcoat soldiers and plagued by midges. His flight took him across the country to Mallaig, for an 80-mile (129km) journey by open boat in a storm to the Outer Hebrides. He came back to Skye disguised as the maidservant of Miss Flora MacDonald. The prince adapted well to the life of a long-distance backpacker, living for weeks in the same dirty shirt and greasy black kilt, growing a long red beard and learning to enjoy the oat bread and whisky of the country. In a bothy on South Uist, he out-drank all of his companions and then proceeded to intone a penitential psalm over their unconscious bodies.

In the face of the weather and a barbarous and implacable enemy, he showed not just strength and courage, but good humour as well. He made jokes with Flora MacDonald – 'they'll never guess what I've got hidden up my skirts' (it was a pistol).

The prince came to know Scotland like no monarch before or since, and at the same time, Scotland's people – from clan chieftains to crofters and fishermen, and even outlaws like the Seven Men of Glenmoriston. Despite a price on his head of £30,000, equivalent to more than a lottery jackpot of today, not one of them betrayed him.

Back on the mainland, in July he was encircled by Hanoverian soldiers, but slipped between two sentries in the dark. By mid-August the manhunt had been abandoned. Soon afterwards he heard of a French boat waiting near Mallaig. Travelling away from the main roads, on 18 September he passed along the route of the walk, up to Coire Ardair and then through the high pass alongside Creag Meagaidh into the empty country around Glen Roy. That pass is called Uinneag Coire Ardair. Translating it into English we can say that Prince Charlie left Scotland through the Window.

WALK 21 DIRECTIONS

1 A new path runs alongside the grey gravel track, leading to Aberarder farm. Here there's an information area and a bench under a roof. Pass to the right of the buildings following a footprint waymarker on to a rebuilt path.

2 The well-built path rises through bracken, then crosses a boggy area. It heads up the valley of Allt Coire Ardair, keeping a little way up the right-hand side, becoming steeper as it ascends through an area of regenerating birch trees. Now the crags of Coire Ardair come into sight ahead. The path crosses many small streams – here it is still being reconstructed. It bends left, slightly downhill, to join the main river. Tiny rowan trees can be seen attempting to regenerate among the heather. Wild flowers in the boggy ground include the pink or white pyramids of the heath spotted orchid (the leaves have the spots). The path winds gently near the stream, then suddenly to the outflow of Lochan a'Choire.

WHILE YOU'RE THERE

The Highland Folk Museum at Newtonmore is the site of Baile Gean, a working reconstruction of an 18th-century township where you can immerse yourself in the peat reek of a traditional black house with heather-thatched roof and smoke-stained walls. The site is so large that a number of pre-war buses take you round it.

WHERE TO EAT AND DRINK

Scotland has few pubs, and the traditional drinking place has always been the bar of the local hotel. Laggan's Monadhliath Hotel caters mainly for locals, but serves bar and restaurant meals to visitors too (children and dogs welcome). It's a former manse, easily recognised by the ruined church in its garden.

❸ The outflow is a fine viewpoint for the crag walls of Coire Ardair. These walls are too loose and overgrown for rock climbing, but when covered in snow and hoarfrost give excellent sport for winter mountaineers. The circuit of the lochan is considerably more rugged than the path up the glen, and could be omitted if the outflow stream is too full, or if a picnic is preferred. Cross the outflow stream near where it emerges from the lochan and follow a trace of path round the shore to the notable clump of

boulders marked by a stretcher box. (The stretcher is used for removing mountain casualties from the foot of the crags.) One of the boulders forms a small cave, with a spring running through it. A vigorous rowan tree, seeded where deer can't get at it, shows that without grazing pressure this glen would be wooded even at this altitude of 2,000ft (610m).

❹ After the boulder cave you must cross rocks and scree. This short section is awkward. Once past the head of the lochan, slant up away from the shore. A path descends from high on the left, coming out of the notch called the Window. Join this and turn down to the loch's outflow (Point **❸** again). Quite clearly there's no way out of this dead-end valley that doesn't involve serious mountain walking – or one of those winter climbs up the icy gullies. Return down the valley by the outward path.

WHAT TO LOOK OUT FOR

The natural forest of the lower slopes of Scotland is the birch. In Creag Meagaidh Reserve, deer numbers are being carefully controlled by shooting to allow the woodland to regenerate without the use of fencing. Early on the path, a signboard shows the treeless slopes as they were in 1986 – they're greener now. Further up, the path passes through young birches. These end quite suddenly at the top of the steeper section. Further up the corrie, just a few tiny rowans can be found struggling out of the heather.

Up and Down the Corrieyairack

Above the Great Glen on the road the English built and Bonnie Prince Charlie marched over.

> DISTANCE 7.25 miles (11.7km)   MINIMUM TIME 4hrs
>
> ASCENT/GRADIENT 1,300ft (396m) ▲▲▲   LEVEL OF DIFFICULTY +++
>
> PATHS Tracks, one vanished pathless section, 2 stiles
>
> LANDSCAPE Foothills of Monadhliath, birchwood hollows
>
> SUGGESTED MAP OS Explorer 400 Loch Lochy & Glen Roy
>
> START/FINISH Grid reference: NH 378080
>
> DOG FRIENDLINESS Off lead, unless passing sheep
>
> PARKING Southern edge of Fort Augustus, signed lane leads off A82 to burial ground
>
> PUBLIC TOILETS Fort Augustus

The most striking feature of Scotland's geography is the 2,000ft (610m) deep Great Glen. It runs perfectly straight from Fort William to Inverness as if a giant ploughshare had been dragged across the country.

Scotland's San Andreas

Around 400 million years ago, the northern part of Scotland slipped 65 miles (105km) to the left. Looking across from Corrieyairack you'd have seen ground that's now the Island of Mull. The Great Glen represents a tear-fault, similar to the San Andreas Fault in California, but no longer active, so that there isn't going to be any Fort Augustus Earthquake. Where two ground masses slide past each other, the rock where they touch is shattered. Rivers and glaciers have worn away this broken rock to make the striking valley.

Wade's Ways

After the uprising of 1715, General Wade became the military commander of Scotland. He constructed and repaired forts along the Great Glen at Fort William, Fort Augustus and Inverness, as well as at Ruthven on the present A9 and Glenelg (see Walk 31). To link them, he built 260 miles (418km) of roads across the Highlands. The most spectacular of these was the one through the Corrieyairack Pass, rising to 2,500ft (762m) to link the Great Glen with the Spey. The construction was little changed since Roman times. Large rocks were jammed together into a firm bed, up to 15ft (4.6m) wide, and then surfaced with smaller stones and gravel packed down. Modern path-builders know that however well you build it, if it's got water running down it, it turns into a stream. Wade paid particular attention to drainage. The 500 soldiers working through the summer of 1731 got a bonus of 6d a day – about £5 in today's money – and celebrated its completion with a barbecue of six oxen.

The chieftains worried that the roads would soften their people, making them unfit for raids across rough country. But they soon came to appreciate

FORT AUGUSTUS

the convenience. 'If you'd seen these roads before they were made, You'd lift up your hands and bless General Wade.'

And when Prince Charles Stuart landed 14 years later, it was the Jacobite army that marched triumphantly across the Corrieyairack. At the Speyside end of the pass, a small and ill-prepared force under General John Cope fled before him into England. And a new Wade rhyme was inserted, temporarily, into the National Anthem itself: 'God grant that Marshal Wade, May by Thy mighty aid, Victory bring, May he sedition hush, and like a torrent rush, Rebellious Scots to crush, God save the King.'

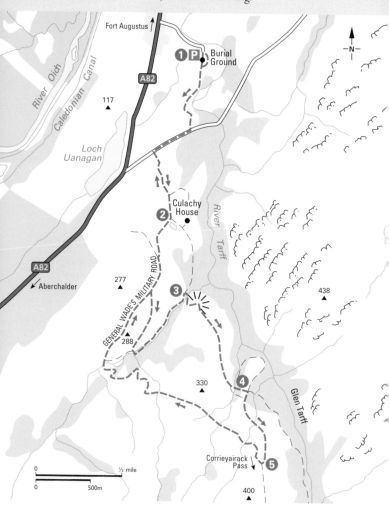

WALK 22 DIRECTIONS

1 A track leads round to the left of the burial ground to meet a minor road. Turn right for about 0.25 mile (400m) to the foot of a rather rubbly track signposted for the Corrieyairack Pass. After some 50yds (46m) the track passes through a gate. It gets much easier at this point and, soon, the right of way joins a smoother track coming up from the pink-coloured Culachy House.

FORT AUGUSTUS

2 After another 0.25 mile (400m), a gate leads out on to the open hill. About 350yds (320m) further on, the track passes under high-tension wires. At once bear left across a grassy meadow. As this drops towards a stream, you will see a green track slanting down to the right. Bear left off the track to pass the corner of a deer fence, where a small path continues down to the stream. Cross and turn downstream on an old grassy track. It recrosses the stream and passes under the high power line to a bend with a sudden view across deep and wooded Glen Tarff.

WHILE YOU'RE THERE

You will find a rather specialised take on the life of the Highlanders at the Clansman Centre in Fort Augustus, which focuses on their techniques of doing away with one another. In a simulated turf house, staff will teach the 'art of killing or maiming using ancient weapons', and will even make the weapons.

3 Turn right across a high stone bridge. A disused track climbs through birch woods then, as a terraced shelf, crosses the high side of Glen Tarff. A side stream forms a wooded re-entrant ahead. The old track contours in to this and crosses below a narrow waterfall – the former bridge has now disappeared.

WHERE TO EAT AND DRINK

The Lock Inn at Fort Augustus is not misspelled: its upstairs restaurant (April–October) overlooks the locks of the Caledonian Canal. Bar meals are served downstairs, year round. Children welcome, but not dogs.

4 Contour out across the steep slope to pick up the old track as it restarts. It runs gently uphill to a gateless gateway in a fence. Turn up the fence to another gateway, 150yds (137m) above. Here turn left for 20yds (18m) to the brink of another stream hollow. (Its delightful Gaelic name – Sidhean Ceum na Goibhre – means 'Fairy Goat-step'.) Don't go into this, but turn uphill alongside it, through pathless bracken, to its top. A deer fence is just above; turn left alongside it to go through a nearby gate, then left beside the fence. When it turns downhill, a green path continues ahead, gently uphill through heather. Far ahead and above, pylons crossing the skyline mark the Corrieyairack Pass. The path bends right to join the Corrieyairack track just above.

WHAT TO LOOK OUT FOR

Despite the road's preservation, you will see little of General Wade's work, apart from its ambitious uphill line preserved by the modern track on top. You may be more interested in the burial ground at the start of the walk. Here is buried 'John Anderson, my Jo', subject of a poem by Robert Burns; and Gilleasbuig MacDonald, bard of North Uist, who died on his way to his publisher in Inverness.

5 Turn right. The track passes a knoll on the right and this heathery rise marks the highest point of this walk. It then descends in sweeping curves for 1.25 miles (2km). The pass is still technically a road, and it is now a scheduled ancient monument and protected by law. Any person found damaging it will be prosecuted. From here the track climbs gently to rejoin the upward route. At the final bend, a stile offers a short cut through (rather than round) the ancient burial ground.

Moorland on Morrone

*The hill at the back of Braemar gives
a taste of the Cairngorms.*

DISTANCE 6.75 miles (10.9km)   MINIMUM TIME 4hrs 15min

ASCENT/GRADIENT 2,000ft (610m) ▲▲▲   LEVEL OF DIFFICULTY +++

PATHS *Well-made but fairly steep path, track, 1 stile*

LANDSCAPE *Rolling heather hills*

SUGGESTED MAP *OS Explorer 387 Glen Shee & Braemar*

START/FINISH *Grid reference: NO 143911*

DOG FRIENDLINESS *Keep on lead in reserve, also on hill during grouse
nesting May/June*

PARKING *Duck pond, at top of Chapel Brae, Braemar*

PUBLIC TOILETS *Braemar centre (opposite Fife Arms)*

Coming down the back of Morrone Hill, you descend through several plant zones, and the home of two distinctive Grampian birds.

Ptarmigan Pterritory

On the windswept, often snow-covered summit plateau, gravel alternates with shrubby plants that grow barely ankle-high. These are food for the ptarmigan, a member of the grouse family that's rather like a small hen. Uniquely among British birds it turns white in the winter, and in spring and early summer it will still be white in patches. Its late summer plumage is paler than the grouse, and more speckled. But the easy way to recognise it is by where it lives – a grouse above the heather line is a ptarmigan – and by its behaviour. It relies on camouflage, and when you notice it, will probably be standing on the gravel only a few yards away. Even then, it doesn't fly away, but will probably wander off round the back of a boulder. In springtime, the male bird's soaring display flight is accompanied by a soundtrack of belches and cackles. The 'P' at the beginning of its name is purely ornamental – in Gaelic it's 'tarmachan'.

Heather and Grouse

At the 2,000ft (610m) mark, bilberry and some grass grow, along with dwarf heather. Once you reach slightly more sheltered ground, the heather springs up twice as high. At around 1,500ft (457m), it is deep enough to hinder off-path walking. Wild flowers like yellow tormentil and white woodruff grow, and you may see meadow pipits and mountain hare.

A small brown bird – or more likely three or four – leaps up out of the heather with a squawking cry that seems to say 'go back, go back!' Grouse go with heather, like pandas go with bamboo and koalas with gum trees. Red grouse are found only in the British Isles, and unfortunately their heather country, however familiar and tiresome to Scottish walkers, is rare and vanishing in a world context. The grouse need old leggy heather to nest in, but shorter, younger plants to eat. As a result, grouse moors are burnt in a ten-year cycle to provide tall heather with short heather. The piebald effect of 'muirburn', as it's called, gives these hills an attractive texture.

Eighty per cent of the grouse's diet is heather, the rest being the insects that live in it. As birds lack teeth they require small stones in their gizzards to help grind their food up and aid digestion. For grouse, sharp quartz grit is ideal, and you may spot small piles of this beside the track.

WALK 23 DIRECTIONS

❶ Take the wide track uphill, to the right of the duck pond at the top of Chapel Brae, bearing left twice following blue waymarkers to Woodhill house. The house can be bypassed by taking a small footpath on the right which rejoins the track just above. When the track forks again, bear left to a viewpoint indicator.

2 Cross a track diagonally to a hill path marked 'Morrone'. The path has been rebuilt with rough stone steps. Higher up, it slants to the right along a line of rocky outcrops, a geological dyke of harder rock. At the top of this it turns directly uphill, passing five sprawling cairns. These are the turning point in the Morrone Hill Race that is part of the Braemar Games. The wide, stony path runs up to the radio mast and other ugly constructions on top of the summit.

WHERE TO EAT AND DRINK

The Duke of Fife used to own all Braemar west of the River Clunie. The Fife Arms, with the standard hewn pine trunks along its frontage, has a large bar full of hillwalkers (and their dogs, on leads). Bar meals are served in generous walker-size portions.

3 The summit, if you turn your back on the buildings, has fine views across Deeside to the high Cairngorms. On the main tops, Ben Macdui and Beinn a'Bhuird, snow may show right through the summer. To the east you will see Loch Callater and the White Mount plateau. A notable hump is Cac Carn Beag, one of the summits of Lochnagar. Morrone's

WHAT TO LOOK OUT FOR

The tundra shrubs that grow on the plateau belong to the heather family, but with oval leaves rather than needles. They can be distinguished easily from August as their berries are conveniently colour-coded. The crowberry fruit is black, the cowberry red and the bilberry, also known as whortleberry and blaeberry, has a juicy purple fruit and pale green leaves. Ptarmigan droppings are stained purple with this fruit, which is also tasty to humans.

summit area is bare stones, but if you go past the buildings you'll find the start of a wide track. It runs down to a shallow col and climbs to the cairn on the low summit beyond. Here it bends left towards a lower col, but before reaching it, turns left again down the side of the hill. A gentle zig-zagging descent leads to the road by the Clunie Water.

4 Turn left, alongside the river, for 1.5 miles (2.4km). Ben Avon with its row of summit tors fills the skyline ahead. After a snow gate and golf clubhouse comes a road sign warning of a cattle grid (the grid itself is round the next bend). Here a track, back up to the left, has a blue-topped waymarker pole.

WHILE YOU'RE THERE

Braemar Castle is smaller, older and to some much more attractive than Balmoral. It was an important strong point, replacing the even older ruin alongside the River Clunie just above the bridge. Its surrounding wall is a later improvement, designed to cope with attackers during the age of the musket and underneath there's a pit dungeon for miscreants. The castle is now run by a community trust.

5 Go up between caravans to a ladder stile with a dog flap. A faint path leads up under birches, bearing right and becoming clearer. After a gate in a fence the path becomes quite clear, leading to a Scottish Natural Heritage signboard and blue waymarker at the top of the birchwood. The path becomes a track with a fence on its right and, in 220yds (201m), reaches the viewpoint indicator, Point **2**. From here you can return to the duck pond and the start of the walk.

Morrone Birkwood

Circle Braemar by an ancient woodland and a royal river.
See map and information panel for Walk 23

DISTANCE *5.5 miles (8.8km)*   MINIMUM TIME *2hrs 15min*

ASCENT/GRADIENT *500ft (152m)* ▲▲▲   LEVEL OF DIFFICULTY ✦✦✦

NOTE *When rivers are very full, the lower part of this walk can be flooded*

WALK 24 DIRECTIONS
(Walk 23 option)

From Point ❶ head back towards the village for 350yds (320m). Turn left past a large larch, and keep left down to a car park (Point ❹). Cross down to the River Dee. Turn right, downstream, between the river and a fence. Continue along the riverbank to where the Clunie Water flows in (Point ❸).

Follow the bank over a slippery stone flood barrier and head upstream beside the Clunie. The path becomes quite narrow and awkward, particularly if trodden by cows. After 0.75 mile (1.2km), a footbridge leads across to a car park opposite the Invercauld Hotel (Point ❻).

Turn right towards Braemar village centre. Just before the bridge, Balnellan Road leads in a few steps to the ruins of the Old Braemar Castle. But this route takes the lane on the left just after the bridge, signed to the golf course. After 0.75 mile (1.2km) it crosses a cattle grid to a track on the right (Point ❺).

Follow Walk 23 up to the viewpoint indicator (Point ❷). Bear left to rejoin the main track ahead; in 50yds (46m) it bears left and contours through birchwood with juniper. After a mile (1.6km), the track reaches a gate with a ladder stile alongside (Point ❹).

Don't cross into the plantation ahead, but turn sharp right on a small path with a 'Circular Route' waymarker. It stays close to the plantation fence for 100yds (91m), then bears right for the same distance. Now it bends right again and passes a damper area on the right, which is grass not heather. Opposite this green patch, two smaller paths turn up to the left. They soon join together at the top of a low knoll and continue down towards the Dee across slabs of bare rock (Point ❺), a fine viewpoint and picnic place.

Continue down a slight spur, passing a small pool in the trees on the right, then bearing right. The path now runs level, with the Dee Valley down on its left. Soon the main 'Circular Route' path rejoins from the right and you cross another stream with stepping-stones. The path is wide and clear now to a kissing gate in a deer fence. Further on is a track junction (Point ❻) near the duck pond. Go straight on here to return to the car park.

Balmoral Castle and the Dee

*A walk past Queen Victoria's memorials
to her husband, servants and dogs.*

DISTANCE DISTANCE 4.75 miles (7.7km)   MINIMUM TIME 2hrs 30min

ASCENT/GRADIENT 800ft (244m) ▲▲▲   LEVEL OF DIFFICULTY ✦✦✦

PATHS Tracks and paths, no stiles

LANDSCAPE Pine forest and viewpoints above wide river valley

SUGGESTED MAP OS Explorer 388 Lochnagar

START/FINISH Grid reference: NO 264949

DOG FRIENDLINESS On lead in castle grounds

PARKING Large pay-and-display at Crathie Church

PUBLIC TOILETS At start, and Balmoral Castle

NOTE Access available Easter to end July only – Royal Family in residence
from August

WALK 25 DIRECTIONS

From the car park, cross the River Dee to the lodge gateway into Balmoral Castle. You must pay to enter the grounds and can also buy a booklet with a map of the marked walks. Shortly, turn right off the driveway on a track that bends to the left as it reaches the river. After 200yds (183m) a path continues along the riverbank. At a yellow waymarker turn left, past a red pillar box to the cafeteria.

Go along to the left of the castle to its far end (the east front).

WHILE YOU'RE THERE
Entering the castle grounds, you've already paid to visit the indoor displays. Victoria and Albert liked to combine tartan wallpaper with tartan floors and decorate with thistles. This was criticised even at the time and has now been moderated. Even so, the pictures are interesting for their Victorian gusto and touch of vulgarity.

This has a plaque of St Hubert, patron saint of hunters. Hubert's message is actually to spare the deer, though this was lost on Prince Albert. A path runs directly away from the castle, to the right of a sunken rose garden, past the memorials to dogs. At a path junction, turn right through a pinewood to regain the riverside.

Turn left on the riverside path. The tall white flowers of angelica grow here, as do lupins, whose seeds are carried here by the river. The path runs up to a tarred driveway, which you follow for 55yds (50m) to a path rising on the left. This crosses another driveway and rises through the woods to a junction with a map showing the estate paths.

Turn up to the right on a track that steepens and bends to the left under larches. At its highest point it reaches a T-junction.

Turn right for the fine view ahead into the corrie of Lochnagar. This mountain dominates Balmoral. It was a favourite of Queen Victoria and the setting for Prince Charles' children's book *The Old Man of Lochnagar* (1980).

The little-used track runs down to join an unsurfaced forest road, where you turn left. A deer fence on the right is threaded with thin laths, designed to make it visible to capercaillie. Injury from flying into fences is a significant reason for the decline of this handsome large grouse, now slowly recovering from near extinction.

After a gate in the deer fence, turn right at a triangle junction, up a new forest road. In about 350yds (320m), a wide path turns up to the left and leads to a huge pyramidal cairn. It was raised 'to the beloved memory of Albert the great and good; prince consort. Erected by his broken-hearted widow'. Victoria and six of her children placed stones bearing their initials in its base. It has wide views in many directions, though not to the castle itself, which is concealed by trees.

The path continues on the right, descending quite steeply to a corner where trees have been felled to provide a view down the Dee. Queen Victoria raised ugly stonework even on supposedly joyous occasions, and the next cairn, massive and conical, celebrates the marriage of her daughter, Princess Beatrix, to Prince Henry of Battenberg. The path descends through the deer fence to a tarred estate road. Opposite is a rather gaudy dry

drinking trough, commemorating General Sir Thomas Myddelton Biddulph KCB.

Turn down the road to the tiny settlement of Easter Balmoral. You can turn left to revisit the castle, as the route is about to leave the estate by turning right across a stream and down left to a public road alongside the Dee.

Turn right, then left, to a white suspension bridge across the river. Follow the road ahead, until a side road on the left leads to Crathie cemetery. Here are 17th-century tombs with death's heads and epitaphs, and the grave of Queen Victoria's special friend, the ghillie John Brown. Interest in Brown has been increased by the film *Mrs Brown* starring Billy Connolly and Judi Dench. Brown's grave was inscribed by his Queen 'that friend on whose fidelity you count, that friend given you by circumstances beyond your control, was God's own gift.' It lies midway between the ruined chapel and the south wall of the kirkyard.

The side road continues to the information centre at the end of the car park.

WHAT TO LOOK FOR
Look out for statues of animals on the walk – a chamois, a wild boar and a collie. The castle also has some odd outbuildings, including green wooden sentry boxes and a circular game larder decorated with antlers.

WALK 26

Crombie Water and the Whisky Hills

A walk through a green valley and bare heather moor in the smugglers' country of Glenlivet.

DISTANCE 6.25 miles (10.1km) **MINIMUM TIME** 3hrs 15min

ASCENT/GRADIENT 1,000ft (305m) ▲▲▲ **LEVEL OF DIFFICULTY** +++

PATHS Waymarked, muddy and indistinct in places, 11 stiles

LANDSCAPE Birchwoods, heather, rolling hills

SUGGESTED MAP OS Explorer 420 Correen Hills & Glenlivet

START/FINISH Grid reference: NJ 218257

DOG FRIENDLINESS Keep on lead except in plantation

PARKING Track opposite church at Tombae runs up to quarry car park

PUBLIC TOILETS None en route or near by.

NOTE Grouse shooting in August/September – consult Glenlivet Ranger Service at Tomintoul

---

Long before the coming of licensed distilleries, whisky was part of the economy of the Highlands. After the hard work of the barley harvest came the quieter occupation of mashing and distilling. The draff (dregs) from the mash-barrel went to feed the cows, while the spirit itself warmed the crofter through the snows of winter.

As rents came to be paid in money rather than in kind, whisky was an easily transported product for cash. It was also convenient to tax, but this simply meant that the Highlanders moved their operation into the hills. The barley fields of Strathspey, the clear mountain water of the Cairngorms and the convenient smuggling routes to Aberdeen and Inverness made Glenlivet a famous whisky region. Even as his redcoats were hunting the smugglers through the Ladder Hills, King George IV was demanding the illicit Glenlivet by name.

Water, Malt – and Mystery

The old word 'Scotch' is only applied to whisky – the people are 'Scottish' and the language is 'Scots'. And whiskey with an 'e' comes from Ireland or the United States. Barley is the start-point. The grain is allowed to germinate in the warm, damp environment of the malting floor, which converts some of its starch to sugar. The malt is heated, under the pagoda-like copper roof of the malting kiln, then boiled and fermented into the 'mash', a kind of sweet insipid beer. The mash is passed three times through the onion-shaped copper stills and stored in barrels for at least eight years. That's the technical process; the added mystery happens almost by accident. The killing of the malt, traditionally done over a peat fire, adds a smoky aroma, but it's the second-hand sherry barrels used for storage that add the golden colour, much of the flavour and the bite of the oakwood.

Blended whiskies, such as Bells, Teachers and Famous Grouse, are made of cheaper corn spirit with malt whisky mixed in. More serious are the 'single malts', each a product of a named distillery. From Glenlivet comes

GLENLIVET

the Glenlivet itself, and also Tomnavoulin, Tomintoul, Cragganmore and Glenfarclas. These are Speyside malts – smooth and subtle. From the islands of the west come wilder whiskies like Lagavoulin and Talisker, with overtones of peat, seaweed and even old fish crates. An educational tasting session could start in the hotels and whisky shops of Tomintoul.

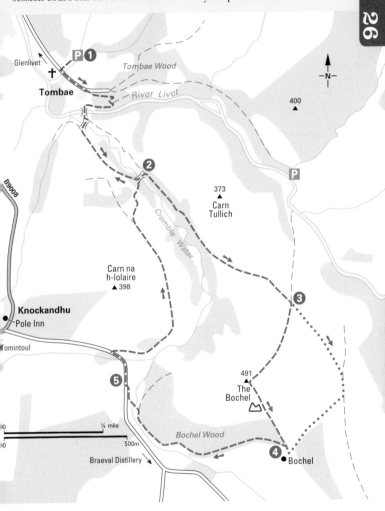

WALK 26 DIRECTIONS

❶ At Tombae church, turn left to walk for 330yds (300m) to a stile on the right – signposted as Walk 10. A track leads down into birchwoods. Bear right at a waymarker and follow the main track to reach a bridge and cross over the River Livet. After 60yds (55m), turn right to another bridge, this time over the Crombie Water. Turn half left, up to a stile beside a field gate. The walk now follows the top of the low wooded bank above the Crombie Water to reach a footbridge.

❷ Across the footbridge, a small path runs across a meadow into a wood, slanting up to the right to a green track. Turn right and follow

GLENLIVET

this gently up through the wood, then bend left on to heather moorland. Below the abrupt hill of The Bochel the track forks. Keep ahead, with a waymarker. The way becomes a peaty path. At the top of the first rise is a stile with a gate alongside. The path, with a waymarker, leads to a gateway in another fence. Don't go through, but turn right, with the fence on your left, to a stile with a signpost.

WHERE TO EAT AND DRINK

At Tomintoul, the highest village in the Highlands, the air is fresh and scented with whisky. Here you'll find that the Glen Avon Hotel does bar meals in the Square, and the Old Firestation Tearoom serves good food and is open all year round.

3 For an easier alternative, follow the sign for Walk 10, ahead. Just before a house, turn right at another signpost and follow a track towards Bochel farm. But the main route goes over The Bochel itself. Across the stile, turn uphill on small sheep paths to the summit cairn. Turn left, to descend towards the white Braeval distillery below the Ladder Hills. As the slope steepens, you'll see Bochel farm below. Head down the left-hand edge of the nearer

pine wood to join the rough track leading into the farm.

4 At once a gate on the right leads to a faint path into the plantation. This soon becomes a green track running just above the bottom edge of the wood. It becomes more well-used and then runs out to a road.

5 Turn right, over a bridge to a waymarked gate on the right. A track rises to open fields above the river. At its highest point, a waymarker points down to the right. Go down to a fence, with a waymarked stile on the left, then through heather with a fence on your left. Turn downhill to a stile at the bottom. Cross this and turn left, ignoring another stile on the left, to reach the footbridge, Point **2**. Retrace the first part of the walk back to Tombae.

WHAT TO LOOK OUT FOR

From the summit of The Bochel, you can see two of Glenlivet's six distilleries. In the north, the Tomnavoulin distillery makes a distinguished Speyside malt. Southwards, the white block of Braeval, currently not operating, used to contribute to blended whiskies. Behind it, faint green lines slanting up the Ladder Hills are the traces of smugglers' paths, where the illicit spirit was carried over to Donside.

Loch an Eilein's Castle and Ord Ban

The castle on the island in the loch is the heart of Rothiemurchus Forest.

DISTANCE 4.25 miles (6.8km)	**MINIMUM TIME** 1hr 45min
ASCENT/GRADIENT 100ft (30m) ▲▲▲	**LEVEL OF DIFFICULTY** +++
PATHS Wide smooth paths, optional steep hill with high ladder stile	
LANDSCAPE Ancient pine forest around loch	
SUGGESTED MAP OS Explorer 403 Cairn Gorm & Aviemore	
START/FINISH Grid reference: NH 897084	
DOG FRIENDLINESS Keep on lead on Rothiemurchus Estate	
PARKING Estate car park near Loch an Eilein, charges apply	
PUBLIC TOILETS Visitor centre	

An island castle, surrounded by ancient pines, and the mountains rising behind – you hardly have to bother with the rest of Scotland, Loch an Eilein has it all.

Castle for Cattle Thieves

Loch an Eilein Castle was built by John Comyn II, known as the Red Comyn, in the 13th century. It guards the strategic cattle-stealing route which runs along the shore of the loch. Locals used to keep a cow tied to a tree in the hope that the raiders would take that and leave the rest alone. The three murderers of a Macintosh chieftain were imprisoned in chains here for seven years, before being executed in 1531. The castle was most recently fought over in 1690, when Grizzel Mhor (Big Grizelda), the chieftain's wife, held it for Clan Grant against the king. There is said to be an underwater zig-zag causeway leading out to the island.

Life in the Pines

Walk quietly with binoculars and you may see some of the unique birdlife of the forest. The crested tit resembles the more familiar coal tit, with brown body and striped head, but its crest has a Mohican hair-style effect. It nests in holes in old, rotten trees, so will only be found in wild forest. The Scottish crossbill, found only in Scotland, has a parrot-like beak, adapted for cracking open pine cones. The capercaillie is the large grouse of the forest and its name means 'horse of the woods'. The male challenges and intimidates other males with a noise like the clip-clop of hooves, or like a wine-bottle being opened. Your only real chance of seeing it in the wild is at dawn, in spring, at the RSPB reserve at Loch Garten (better known for its ospreys).

Osprey Island

Ospreys used to nest in the castle ruins. An egg collector once swam across wearing nothing but his cap, which he used to bring back his plunder. Ospreys are back in the Cairngorms, and though they won't return to this

WALK

27

over-public island, you might see them elsewhere, plunging feet-first as they strike for a trout. Try the trout farm at Inverdruie, on the edge of Aviemore. Sadly, the egg-collectors are back as well. In 2000, a man in Leicester was caught with three stolen osprey eggs.

Romantic Setting

In the romantic novel *The Key above the Door* by Maurice Walsh (1926), the hero and heroine spend half the book gazing at each other from cottages on opposite sides of Loch an Eilein before accidentally getting shipwrecked on the island. More recently, Archie and Katrina, from the popular TV series *Monarch of the Glen*, enjoyed their own romantic encounter on the island.

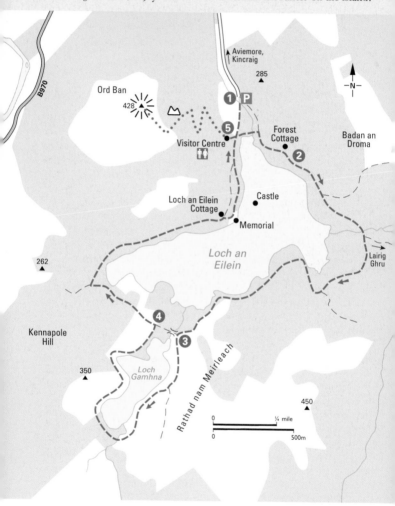

WALK 27 DIRECTIONS

❶ From the end of the car park at the beginning of the walk, a made-up path leads to the visitor

centre. Turn left to cross the end of Loch an Eilein, then turn right on a smooth sandy track. The loch shore is near by on the right. There are small paths leading down to it if you wish to visit. Just past a red-roofed house, a deer fence runs across, with a gate.

2 The track now becomes a wide, smooth path, which runs close to the loch side. After a bridge, the main track forks right to pass a bench backed by a flat boulder. The smaller path on the left leads high into the hills and through the famous pass of the Lairig Ghru, eventually to Braemar. After crossing a stream at a low concrete footbridge, the path bends right for 120yds (110m) to a junction. Just beyond you'll find a footbridge with wooden handrails.

WHAT TO LOOK OUT FOR

At the foot of the loch, you walk across a low loggers' dam. Timber men used to release the water to carry the tree trunks down to the Spey. We usually think of the log-rafts of the great Canadian rivers, but the skill was carried there by Highlanders from Rothiemurchus.

3 To shorten the walk, cross this footbridge and continue along the main track, passing Point **4** in another 170yds (155m). For a longer walk, turn left before the footbridge on to a narrower path that will pass around Loch Gamhna. This second loch soon

WHERE TO EAT AND DRINK

Smiffy's Fish & Chips at Aviemore is celebrated across Scotland by hillwalkers and climbers. For even hungrier ones, La Taverna offers a pizza and salad 'eat as much as you can' buffet, as well as more formal Italian restaurant fare. You can find it at the south end of Aviemore, opposite the turn-off to Glenmore

appears on your right-hand side. Where the path forks, keep right to pass along the loch side, across its head (rather boggy) and back along its further side, to rejoin the wider path around Loch an Eilein. Turn left here.

4 Continue around Loch an Eilein, with the water on your right, to a reedy corner of the loch and a bench. About 55yds (50m) further, the path turns sharply right, signposted 'footpath'. After a gate, turn right to the loch side and a memorial to Major General Brook Rice who drowned here while skating. Follow the shore to the point opposite the castle, then back up to the wide track above. A deer fence on the left leads back to the visitor centre.

5 From here, a stiff climb (500ft/152m) can be made on to the rocky little hill of Ord Ban, a superb viewpoint. Cross a ladder stile immediately to the right of the toilet block and follow the deer fence to the right for 150yds (137m), to a point behind the car park. Just behind one of the lowest birches on the slope, a small indistinct path zig-zags up the steep slope. It slants to the left to avoid crags, then crosses a small rock slab (take care if wet) and continues on to the summit. Descend by the same path.

WHILE YOU'RE THERE

Careful observers might see the wildcat, pine marten and capercaillie, but it's several centuries too late to spot the extinct wolf, bison and lynx. However, all these can be seen at the Highland Wildlife Park at Kincraig. It's an outpost of Edinburgh Zoo, where all the Cairngorms' wildlife past and present is kept under fairly natural conditions.

The Pass of Ryvoan and the Thieves' Road

*Following cattle thieves and drovers to the lochan
used by the fairies for their laundry.*

WALK 28

DISTANCE 5 miles (8km)	**MINIMUM TIME** 2hrs 15min

ASCENT/GRADIENT 400ft (122m) ▲▲▲   **LEVEL OF DIFFICULTY** ✦✦✦

PATHS Smooth tracks, one steep ascent, no stile

LANDSCAPE Views over Rothiemurchus Forest to Cairngorm

SUGGESTED MAP OS Explorer 403 Cairn Gorm & Aviemore

START/FINISH Grid reference: NH 980095

DOG FRIENDLINESS Off lead but under close control

PARKING Bridge just south of Glenmore village

PUBLIC TOILETS Glenmore village

The Pass of Ryvoan has all the atmosphere of a classic Cairngorm through-route. It's a scaled down version of the famous and fearsome Lairig Ghru that cuts through the Cairngorm range southwards from Aviemore. You pass from the shelter of the forest to a green lochan, trapped between two high and stony mountainsides. Once through the narrow gap, you'll find wide moors and a ring of peaks around the horizon.

Thieving Ways

Ryvoan marked the exit of the Thieves' Road that ran out of Rannoch and Lochaber by secret ways through the Rothiemurchus Forest. The MacDonalds of Glen Coe used to come raiding here in the 17th century, as did Clan Cameron from Loch Eil near Fort William. Once through the pass, they could take their pick from the rich lands of Moray and Aberdeenshire. In more settled times, the raiding chieftains became landlords, and their rents were paid in the small black cattle of the glens. Every autumn, the drove herds assembled for their long walk to the markets of Falkirk, Perth and northern England.

The Old Drove Road

The drovers used the same road as their thieving grandfathers, but once through the pass they turned sharp right across the flank of the mountain. The Lairig an Lui, the Pass of the Calves, crosses the dangerous ford of the Avon and runs down Glen Derry to Braemar. It's 30 miles (48km) to the next grazing and shelter – two full days for the drove. Overnight the cattle would snatch some grazing from the rough grasses, while the drovers cooked their oatmeal and potatoes, before rolling themselves in their woollen plaids on a bed of heather. As late as 1859, Queen Victoria found the Lairig path torn up by hooves and scented with fresh cow pats.

The Sithe and Others

Lochan Uaine means 'Green Loch'. Some say the green colour is caused by flecks of mica. Others claim that it's where the fairies wash their green garments. The Highland fairies, the Sithe (pronounced 'Shee'), don't dance around with wands and grant you wishes. They are touchy and vengeful, and if you meet one it is best to address him politely in good Gaelic. Precautions you can take are to avoid wearing green, which is known to annoy them, and never to address your friends by name while under the trees.

The Bodach Lamh-dearg is a spectre who appears wrapped in a grey plaid with one bloodstained hand, challenging passers-by to a fight and leaving their bodies for the foxes. Big Donald, the King of the Fairies, lived beside Loch Morlich.

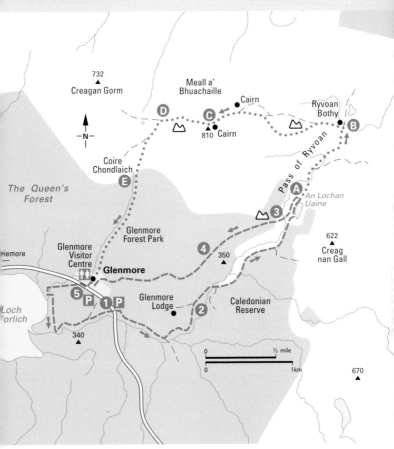

WALK 28 DIRECTIONS

❶ Head upstream on a sandy track to the left of the river. Interpretation signs explain the flowers of the forest you may come across, many of which are ferns and mosses. After 550yds (503m), turn left on a wide smooth path with blue/yellow waymarkers. Ahead is a gate into

Glenmore Lodge rifle range; here the path bends right, to a wide gravel track.

❷ Turn right, away from Glenmore Lodge, to cross a concrete bridge into the Caledonian Reserve. Immediately keep ahead on a smaller track (marked by a blue waymarker) as the main one bends right. The

WALK 28

track narrows as it heads into the Pass of Ryvoan between steep wooded slopes of pine, birch and scree. At this, the most scenic part of the route, a path turns left, with a blue waymarker, which you take in a moment. Just beyond this, steps on the right lead down to Lochan Uaine. Walk round to the left of the water on the beach. At the head of the loch a small path leads back up to the track. Turn sharp left, back to the junction already visited; now turn off to the right on to the narrower path with the blue waymarker.

❸ This small path crosses some duckboard and heads back down the valley. Very soon it starts to climb steeply to the right, up rough stone steps. When it levels off the going is easier, although it's still narrow with tree roots. The path reaches a forest road at a bench and a waymarker.

❹ Continue to the left along the track. After a clear-felled area with views, the track re-enters trees and slopes downhill into Glenmore village. Just above the main road turn right, through a green barrier, to reach Glenmore

Visitor Centre. Pass through its car park to the main road.

WHILE YOU'RE THERE

Reintroduced to the Cairngorms after an absence of around 1,000 years, the Glenmore reindeer herd is based at Glenmore village. From the Reindeer Centre you'll be taken up the hill to visit the herd. Some of the reindeer pull sleighs in Christmas parades.

❺ Cross to Glenmore shop. Behind a post-box, steps lead down to the campsite. Pass along its right-hand edge to a path into woods. Head left across a footbridge to the shore of Loch Morlich and follow the beaches until another river blocks the way. Turn left along the river bank. Ignore a footbridge, but continue on the wide path with the river on your right. Where the path divides, the smaller branch continues beside the river through bushes to the car park.

WHERE TO EAT AND DRINK

The Forestry Commission's visitor centre has a café serving baked potatoes and snacks. Across the road, the Glenmore Café offers chips, toasties and red squirrels – the squirrels are outside, using a feeder placed directly opposite the windows.

WHAT TO LOOK OUT FOR

Elsewhere in Britain, red squirrels are being supplanted by their big grey cousins which were introduced from America. However, the red squirrel's smaller teeth are better adapted to life among the pines, and it is widespread in the Rothiemurchus Forest. Typically they'll run up the side of a tree trunk facing away from you, but then you'll see them escaping through the branches overhead. You may get a close-up view at the Glenmore Café.

Meall a' Bhuachaille

Looking at the Cairngorms from a smallish mountain above the fairy lochan.

See map and information panel for Walk 28

DISTANCE 6.5 miles (10.4km)	MINIMUM TIME 4hrs
ASCENT/GRADIENT 1,700ft (518m) ▲▲▲	LEVEL OF DIFFICULTY ✦✦✦

WALK 29 DIRECTIONS
(Walk 28 option)

Leaving the summit of Meall a' Bhuachaille in mist is tricky, so inexperienced walkers should only attempt this walk in clear weather.

Walk 28 leads to Lochan Uaine. From the loch head (Point **A**), turn right along the track to continue up the valley. The gable of Ryvoan bothy (shepherd's hut) is briefly visible ahead. The track forks; turn left, signed 'Nethy Bridge'. A signboard welcomes you to Abernethy Reserve, and soon you arrive at the bothy (Point **B**).

Here a path turns off to the left, to climb Meall a' Bhuachaille. It has been newly rebuilt, and is smooth with some stepped sections. At the foot of the steeper slope it slants up left, giving views down to Lochan Uaine. After some zig-zags it bends up right, to the top of the steep slope above the bothy.

In Strath Nethy below, pines from the north and the south are about to rejoin. Soon squirrels will hop, branch to branch, from Grantown to Glen Feshie.

The path bends left, and heads up the rounded, heathery crest with the summit about 550yds (503m) beyond. Here you will find a large

cairn (Point **C**), with a circular shelter of low stones. Note that you arrive from the direction of the opening in this shelter.

To leave the summit, pass to the right of the big cairn and head down for 35yds (30m) to where the built path restarts. (The first sign of it is a stone drainage runnel.) It bends left, to run straight down the rounded spur towards a col below. Above this col, the slope eases a little and the path divides (Point **D**). Ignore the path ahead, which becomes peaty as it heads for the col just below. Instead take the main path down to the left as it slants around Coire Chondlaich. The natural treeline here is at 765yds (700m), the altitude of the path junction above, but nibbling deer prevent much of the regrowth that could take place.

Soon the well-built path heads directly downhill, to join a stream. A red-top waymarker is at the top of clear-felled plantations (Point **E**). The path runs down to the left of the stream, with a strip of standing pine left to shelter it.

At a fork and signboard, a smaller path on the right has both red and blue waymarker, and soon arrives at Glenmore village (Point **5** of Walk 28). The starting car park is 0.25 mile (400m) east along the road.

WALK 30

Boat of Garten and the Spey

Along the banks of the great river, with a pinewood return.

DISTANCE 5.75 miles (9.2km) (+ 0.5 mile/0.8km Fairy Hill)

MINIMUM TIME 2hrs 15min

ASCENT/GRADIENT 197ft (60m) ▲▲▲ LEVEL OF DIFFICULTY +++

PATHS Riverside path, wide woodland track, 2 stiles

LANDSCAPE Wide River Spey, pine forest

SUGGESTED MAP OS Explorer 403 Cairn Gorm & Aviemore

START/FINISH Grid reference: NH 945191

DOG FRIENDLINESS Dogs not welcome on riverside – use track on right

PARKING Small pull-in at east of Boat of Garten village, next to bridge

PUBLIC TOILETS Boat of Garten

WALK 30 DIRECTIONS

You can walk out on to Garten Bridge for the upstream view, but return to the village end. Villages with the name 'Boat' are the sites of former ferries. The 1974 concrete bridge replaced a wooden bridge of 1899, which itself replaced the boat. The Osprey Bistro has a picture of the chain ferry and the newly built bridge above it.

At the village end of the bridge, on the upstream side, a small kissing gate is marked 'No Dogs'. It leads to a riverside path upstream. The path, one tree back from the river so as not to disturb the fish and anglers, runs through a wood, where monkey flower is bright yellow in the ditches, and past a golden sandy beach. Rest at one of the benches and you might see a kingfisher. The path now runs along the edge of the riverside field, with views ahead to the high Cairngorms. Giant knapweeds grow here, thistle-like but without the prickles.

The Spey is one of the great rivers of Scotland. It wanders across its wide strath (mountain valley) in great meanders, in the style of a mature river. In fact it's still 650ft (198m) above sea level. At times of storm or snow-melt it became impassable, and it was only after it was bridged, during the early 19th century, that northern Scotland became fully accessible.

For centuries before that, the river was itself a highway for the floaters – the men who brought the logs down out of the forests of the Cairngorms. Today, canoeists have established their own right of navigation in the river.

The riverside path continues through pastureland with gorse. A house blocks the riverside ahead; turn right, at a waymarker and sign, 'Kinchurdy Road', and cross a field to a track. Turn left along the track. It runs parallel to the river, which is nearby on the left, then bends right, into a wood of birches and broom. Where it bends left, a path ahead

BOAT OF GARTEN

WALK 30

(again signed 'Kinchurdy Road') could be used to shorten the walk drastically. The main route keeps on along the track. It rejoins the river at a deep reach of smooth water, and runs through meadows. With the fishing lodge of Kinchurdy ahead, a cattle grid leads out to another stony track.

WHERE TO EAT AND DRINK
The Boat Hotel, in Boat of Garten, is the original station hotel. Its Osprey Bistro and Capercaillie Restaurant serve traditional Scottish food, freshly cooked. It's so popular that for an evening meal you probably need to book. No dogs, but children are welcome.

Turn right, away from the river, through a farm where you take the middle track of three. On the left is Loch Dallas. Follow the track for a mile (1.6km). The Speyside Way joins from the left and, immediately afterwards, the track passes under the granite bridge of the Speyside Steam Railway.

The Speyside Way, Scotland's third long distance path, has finally become continuous from Aviemore to the sea at Spey Bay, with an extension planned upriver to Newtonmore. It uses the former Spey railway for much of its length and is a smooth and level walk – the main difficulty is negotiating the various distilleries alongside the route.

Here, however, the Way has been evicted from its track by the Speyside Steam Railway, reopened

for tourists. It runs through Bridge of Garten to Broomhill, whose station was Glen Bogle in the TV series *Monarch of the Glen*.

Once under the bridge, the main track bends right, signed 'Kinchurdy Road'; instead turn half right on a stony track that veers to the left into pine woods. Continue for 50yds (46m), turning right at a 'Woodland Walks' sign.

A narrower track of earth and stones leads through pine and heather. Once more you're in the regenerating Caledonian Forest. This is described as semi-wild: it was planted fairly recently, but is now being allowed to regenerate of its own accord. Thickets of young trees are thinning themselves by natural wastage, gradually creating a more open style of woodland.

The track passes two more 'Woodland Walks' signposts, where you keep ahead on the main track. At the edge of the village, turn right, again signed 'Woodland Walks', and left past the end of a football pitch. Near Boat of Garten's main street, a further 'Woodland Walks' signpost points to the right, to another junction. (Here a right turn leads to the Fairy Hill, 0.25 mile (400m) away; a resting point with a view in winter when leaves are down.) The path on the left leads between houses to the village street. Turn right and follow the street round two bends to Garten Bridge and the start of the walk.

WHAT TO LOOK FOR
On the left as you approach Boat of Garten is an area of fire damaged forest. Two successive fires here have blackened the trunks and consumed the heather undergrowth, with bilberry now growing in its place, but the trees have survived, losing only their lower branches.

Looking Over the Sea to Skye

A coast walk along Loch Alsh with views of Skye, the sea and a fish farm.

DISTANCE 8.5 miles (13.7km)	MINIMUM TIME 4hrs
ASCENT/GRADIENT 1,000ft (305m) ▲▲▲	LEVEL OF DIFFICULTY +++
PATHS Tracks, grassy shoreline, minor road, 4 stiles	
LANDSCAPE Wooded coast, moorland pass, stony paths	
SUGGESTED MAP OS Explorer 413 Knoydart, Loch Hourn & Loch Duich	
START/FINISH Grid reference: NG 795213	
DOG FRIENDLINESS Off lead most of walk	
PARKING Above pier of Glenelg ferry	
PUBLIC TOILETS None en route or near by	

Two hundred years ago, Scotland's rivers were full of salmon, and smoked salmon was the crofter's winter food store. When wild salmon became scarce it was considered a luxury food, and today, if you buy salmon, it's almost certainly from a fish farm.

Fish Farming

A fish farm should be sheltered from storm waves, but in water at least 30ft (9m) deep so that fish droppings don't poison the fish. There should be a vigorous tidal flow to carry oxygen-rich water into the pens, no pollution and the water should be cool, but should not freeze. In other words, it should be in a Scottish sea loch. Scotland's farms now produce salmon with a fish-counter value of one billion pounds each year, they employ 8,500 people and produce 160,000 tonnes of fish a year, enough to give every Briton a 4oz (100g) steak every week.

Fish farming is a tough life. Mending a net that's 3ft (90cm) underwater is not comfortable when the water is still, and it invariably isn't, because the day when it's blowing half a gale is the very day the nets break. Hauling the cages out of the water for cleaning is the toughest job of all – seaweed grows on fish farms just as it does on the shoreline, and after two years it starts to hinder the flow of water. And a single storm, or even a passing whale, can tear the nets and lose the work of two years.

Mass Catering

During its first 40 years, fish farming tried to produce as much as possible, as cheaply as possible. Salmon were stocked like battery hens and fed a high-fat diet. Antibiotics keep them alive if not altogether healthy, and dyes give their flesh the pink colour. One result has been pollution from their droppings poisoning nearby shellfish beds. Fish farms act as reservoirs of disease, in particular of the parasitic sea-lice. There are many reasons for the decline of the wild salmon and infection from fish farms is one of them.

Scottish fish farming has now reached the point where it has to clean up its act. A recent development is the organic fish farm, where the fish are stocked less densely and are fed a more natural diet. Fish pens are circular because the salmon prefer to swim round and round. If they were put in a square enclosure, the corners would be wasted. More importantly, the fish would hit the sides, and this would damage their scales.

WALK 31 DIRECTIONS

1 A track runs out of the car park, signed for Ardintoul and Totaig. It descends gently through two gates, then goes up through a third into a plantation. With high power lines just above, the track

forks. Take the left-hand one, downhill, passing an arrow made of stones. The track runs between the feet of a tall pylon and then climbs again to contour through a birch wood. It runs in and out of a tiny stream gorge, then gently descends towards the shore.

GLENELG

On the other side of Loch Alsh, the white houses of Balmacara are directly ahead.

❷ At the shoreline, the track disappears into an open field strip. Follow the short grass next to the shingle beach, passing a salmon farm just offshore. When the trees once more run down to the sea, a green track runs next to the shore to reach an open field below a small crag with birches. Keep along the shore, outside field walls, and sometimes taking to the stripy schist shingle, towards a square brick building on the point ahead. As you pass the end of the birch crag, you come to a wall gap. Here a track that's simply a pair of green ruts runs directly inland through a grey gate to meet

a gravel track. Turn left, away from the abandoned Ardintoul farm to pass sheds and a house to regain the shoreline at Ardintoul.

❸ The track runs along the shoreline, then turns inland to climb the hill behind. The steeper uphill sections are tarred. Below on the left, the Allt na Dalach runs into Loch Alsh, with, at low tide, a clear example of a gravel spit where river debris runs into tidal water. The track enters plantations, crosses a stream and bends right to complete its climb to the Bealach Luachrach. Here you may see fresh peat workings on the left.

❹ The energetic can make a diversion on to Glas Bheinn – a tough little hill, but a fine viewpoint. The grading and timing given for this walk don't take account of this side-trip. From the road's high point, turn right up a wet tree gap to reach open hillside. Follow the remains of an old fence up the first rise. Where it bends right, continue straight uphill to the summit, returning by the same route. The old fence makes a useful guide back into the tree gap. Continue downhill from Point ❹ on the unsurfaced road, which reaches the tarred public road a mile (1.6km) north of Glenelg village. Grassy shoreline, then the road, leads back to the ferry pier.

Heart of the Cuillins

*Classic rock-climbing country below the
Chioch and the Inaccessible Pinnacle.*

DISTANCE 5.75 miles (9.2km)   **MINIMUM TIME** 4hrs

ASCENT/GRADIENT 1,900ft (580m) ▲▲▲   **LEVEL OF DIFFICULTY** +++

PATHS Mountain paths, one boggy and tough, 2 stiles

LANDSCAPE Peaty slopes into spectacular crag hollow

SUGGESTED MAP OS Explorer 411 Skye – Cuillin Hills

START/FINISH Grid reference: NG 409206

DOG FRIENDLINESS Signs indicate lead use in sheep country below corrie

PARKING Walkers' pull-in before gate into Glenbrittle campsite

PUBLIC TOILETS Glenbrittle campsite

The Black Cuillin Hills, seen through Skye's moist Atlantic air, appear blue and under romantic sunset light almost purple. This land is like nowhere else, even in Scotland, for crag, boulder and jagged horizon.

The Glory of Gabbro

The special quality of Skye is obvious to the eye, but even more so to the foot. The black rock grips the foot like velcro. This is gabbro, formed in the magma chamber of a volcano about the height of Mount Fuji that stood here 50 million years ago. Skye's screes are the steepest, its crags the craggiest, and its ridges look out across the Hebrides and the Atlantic.

As you approach Point ❹ on the upward journey, you are looking towards the buttress of Sron na Ciche. High on the face is a smooth, diamond-shaped slab and, at its right-hand corner, a famous rock-projection. It long went unnoticed, until a famous climber, Professor Norman Collie, spotted the shadow it casts across the slab in the afternoon. This is A'Chioch, 'the Breast'. Its flat top was the scene of a sword-fight in the film *Highlander*. The top is reached by a spectacular, but fairly straightforward climb.

Behind Lagan

In the upper corrie, more famous bits of rock come into view. At the back right corner is the long scree called the Great Stone Shoot. It is strenuous and frustrating but not technically difficult, and it brings climbers up to the ridge just to the right of Skye's highest peak, Sgurr Alasdair. The skyline to the left of the Stone Shoot is dominated by Sgurr Mhic Choinnich, with its near-vertical right profile. This step, 200ft (61m) high, can be avoided by a remarkable ledge that crosses below the summit, to emerge on the mountain's gentler left-hand ridge.

To the left again, you can just see the rock-prow of the so-called Inaccessible Pinnacle. This forms the summit of Skye's second highest peak, Sgurr Dearg. Its easiest route is very scary, but only moderately difficult and not particularly inaccessible. It must be climbed by anyone wishing to complete the Munro summits, Scottish peaks over 3,000ft (914m).

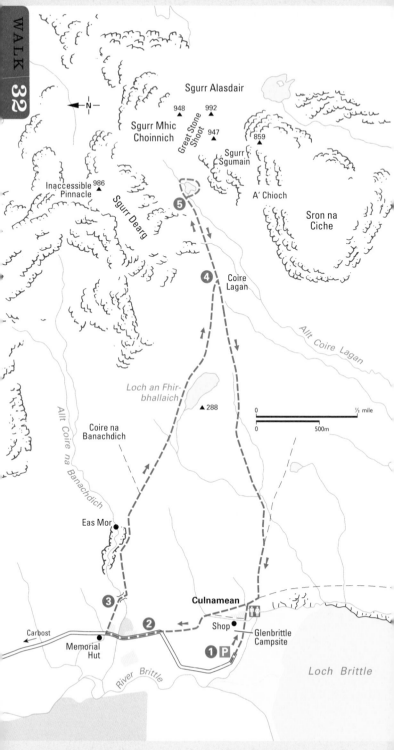

Sgurr Alasdair

948 ▲   992 ▲

Sgurr Mhic
Choinnich

947 ▲

Great Stone Shoot

Sgurr
Sgumain

859 ▲

A' Chioch

←—N—

Inaccessible 986 ▲
Pinnacle

Sron na
Ciche

Sgurr
Dearg

5

Coire
Lagan

4

Allt Coire Lagan

Loch an Fhir-
bhallaich

▲ 288

Coire na
Banachdich

0 ——————— ½ mile
0 ——————— 500m

Culnamean

Eas Mor ●

Allt Coire na Banachdich

Shop ●

3

2

Glenbrittle
Campsite

← Carbost

Memorial
Hut ●

1 P

River Brittle

Loch Brittle

WALK 32 DIRECTIONS

1 From the parking area, the track leads on through Glenbrittle campsite to a gate with a kissing gate. Pass left of the toilet block to cross a stile. Turn left along a stony track just above, which runs gently downhill above the campsite, to rejoin the Glenbrittle road.

2 Keep ahead to cross a bridge with the white Memorial Hut just ahead. On the right are some stone buchts (sheep-handling enclosures) and here a waymarked path heads uphill to reach a footbridge which crosses the Allt Coire na Banachdich.

3 Cross the footbridge and head up to the right of the stream's deep ravine, with a great view of the waterfall at its head. Its Gaelic name, Eas Mor, means simply 'Big Waterfall'. Above, the path bears right, to slant up the hillside. Below the spur of Sgurr Dearg, the path forks. Here keep right, aiming for the right-hand of the two corries above, which is Coire Lagan. The path passes above Loch an Fhir-bhallaich. After a short steepening, the rebuilding works currently end and the path becomes rough. It rounds a shoulder into the lower part of Coire Lagan and meets a much larger path at a big cairn.

4 Turn uphill on this path, until a belt of bare rock blocks the way into the upper corrie. This rock has been smoothed by a glacier into gently-rounded swells, known as 'boiler-plates'. A scree field runs up into the boiler-plate rocks. The best way keeps up the left edge, below a slab wall with a small waterslide, to the highest point of the scree. Head up left for 50ft (15m) on bare rock, then back right on ledges to an eroded scree above the boiler-plate obstruction. Look back down your upward route to note it for your return. The trodden way slants up to the right. With the main stream near by on the right, it goes up to the rim of the upper corrie.

5 The boiler-plate slabs at the lochan's outflow are excellent for picnics. Walking mainly on bare rock, it's easy to make a circuit of the lochan. For the return journey, retrace your steps to Point **4**. Ignoring the right fork of the route you came up by, keep straight downhill on the main path. It runs straight down to the toilets at Glenbrittle campsite. Turn left over a rustic footbridge to finish along the beach.

Overleaf: The Cuillin Hills looking across Loch Scavaig from Elgol, Isle of Skye (Walk 32)

Prison and Pinnacle

*Exploring the weird lava landscape
of Skye's northern peninsula.*

WALK 33

DISTANCE 5.25 miles (8.4km)   **MINIMUM TIME** 3hrs

ASCENT/GRADIENT 1,200ft (366m) ▲▲▲   **LEVEL OF DIFFICULTY** ✦✦✦

PATHS Well-used path, 2 stiles

LANDSCAPE Rock towers and pinnacles

SUGGESTED MAP OS Explorer 408 Skye – Trotternish & the Storr

START/FINISH Grid reference: NG 440679

DOG FRIENDLINESS Keep on lead passing sheep, take care on cliff top

PARKING Lay-by, top of pass on Staffin–Uig road. Overflow parking at cemetery 0.25 mile (400m) on Staffin side (not available during funerals)

PUBLIC TOILETS Brogaig

The rocks of Scotland vary from ancient – about 400 million years – to a great deal older than that, but along the western edge is something quite different. The great eye of the Atlantic Ocean opened at a time that, geologically speaking, is this morning just before breakfast. A mere 60 million years ago, the mid-Atlantic ridge lay just off the Scottish coast. And all along that ridge, new seabed emerged in exotic and interesting volcanic rocks that now form the Arran granite, the basalt of Mull and Skye, and the Skye gabbro.

Lava Landscape

Stir together butter and sugar in a saucepan, take the mixture off the heat and it crystallises into fudge. But take the same ingredients and cool them quickly, by tipping them into cold water, for example, and you get the glassy solid we call toffee. Now take a basic silicaceous magma, let it cool over thousands of years deep inside a volcano, and you'll get the rough crystalline gabbro that featured on Walk 32. But let it erupt suddenly at the surface, and it congeals into basalt, which is black, shiny and slippery. It forms a completely different sort of scenery – that of northern Skye.

Basalt lava is a slippery liquid, like milk rather than treacle. This makes it quite different from the lumpy rhyolite lava that formed Glen Coe and the craggy side of Ben Nevis. Basalt lava spreads in wide, shallow layers across the country. After erosion, you get a flat-topped landscape, with long low cliffs at the edges and wide grassy plateaux. Macleod's Tables and Dun Caan on Raasay (see Walk 36) are lava-layer hills.

North of Portree, the lava flowed out over older, softer rocks of Jurassic (dinosaur) age. All along the Trotternish peninsula, the sea has been steadily removing those softer rocks, and the basalt above has been breaking off in hill-sized chunks and slipping downhill and eastwards. The chunks lean over, split apart and erode: the result is some extraordinary scenery, of which the queerest is the Quiraing. Some of its rock forms, with intriguing names such as The Prison, The Needle and the Fingalian Slab, have been

QUIRAING

a tourist must-see since Victorian times. As a result, a wide, well-made path leads below these pinnacles, then back along the top. Here you will find a gently undulating lawn, which would be quite suitable for a spot of croquet, that's called The Table. Spread your picnic cloth on The Table, and then peep out between the rock architecture to the Sound of Raasay and the distant hills of Torridon.

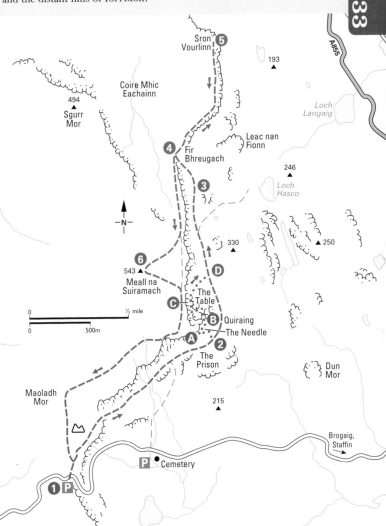

WALK 33 DIRECTIONS

1 A well-built path starts at a small green signpost opposite the lay-by, where you can park. The jagged tower of grass and rock on the skyline is The Prison. The path crosses over the steep landslip slope towards it, with an awkward crossing of a small stream gully on bare rock and then passes a small waterfall high above and heads to the right, rather than up into a rocky gap. It turns uphill into the wide col to the left of The Prison.

WHAT TO LOOK OUT FOR

Basalt rock is alkaline and relatively rich in lime and minerals, so its soils support meadow flowers such as would more usually be seen in the English countryside. Yellow rattle, a flower of ancient pastureland, has been spotted here. Sron Vourlinn grows daisies like any suburban lawn. Global warming has encouraged the marbled white butterfly, blotchy brown and white, to move north from England as well.

2 The main path does not drop, but goes forward, slightly uphill, crossing a new fence at a stile and then dodging below a crag foot. It crosses the foot of steep ground, then passes above a small peat pool. Ignore a path forking down right; the main path slants up to the left into a col where an old wall runs across.

3 The path descends into a landslip valley that runs across rather than down the hillside, then slants up left to a col with a stile.

4 Cross and turn right for the excursion to Sron Vourlinn. Follow the crest over a slightly rocky section with a short descent beyond, then join the main path along a grassy meadow with a very

WHILE YOU'RE THERE

Kilt Rock is seen from a clifftop viewpoint at Staffin. The warning (in Gaelic and five other languages) not to climb over the fence seems scarcely necessary as immediately beyond is a 500ft (152m) drop to the sea. Lean over to see the startling waterfall and columnar basalt cliff. Some of the six-sided blocks have fallen off and lie in the sea directly below the platform.

sudden edge on the right. After the highest point, continue slightly downhill to the north top. Here you can see that the land is still slipping, with a crevasse beside the cliff edge where another narrow section is shortly to peel away. The shelter of the rock crevice grows rock rose, rowan and valerian.

WHERE TO EAT AND DRINK

The Pieces of Ate café at Brogaig, at the foot of the hill road, serves home-made snacks and soup from a small shack (closed on Sundays, as is most of the island). Magnificently sited below the Quiraing crags, the Flodigarry Hotel offers evening meals and Sunday lunch at its restaurant, bistro and terrace, specialising in local lobster and other seafood.

5 Return to the col with the stile (Point **4**) and continue uphill. The drops are now on your left, as you look down towards the pinnacles surrounding The Table. After passing broken ground on the right, you come to a fallen wall, part of which appears from below as a cairn. The path continues next to the cliff edge on the left; you can fork off right, directly uphill, to the summit trig point on Meall na Suiramach.

6 Follow a broad faint path slightly downhill to a cairn at the cliff edge. You now look straight down on to The Table, 100ft (30m) below. Turn right on the wide path alongside the crag drop. After 0.25 mile (400m) as the path steepens, you'll see a fence on your right with a kissing gate. Once through this, the path becomes much clearer, contouring across the steep slope of Maoladh Mor. Above the car park, it turns straight downhill for a final ascent.

Climbing on The Table

Threading behind the Needle where the MacDonalds hid their cattle.
See map and information panel for Walk 33

DISTANCE 5.75 miles (9.2km)	MINIMUM TIME 4hrs
ASCENT/GRADIENT 1,800ft (548m) ▲▲▲	LEVEL OF DIFFICULTY +++

WALK 34 DIRECTIONS
(Walk 33 option)

From Walk 33 you can make a short but strenuous diversion to The Table. This takes you into the heart of the bizarre rock formations above the secret stronghold where the people of Staffin hid their cattle; the Gaellic name Quiraing means a round cattle enclosure.

A sprawling cairn stands in the col (Point ❷), with a jumble of crags and towers above, most noticeably the pointed pinnacle of The Needle. An eroded path zig-zags up the steep slope towards it, then up to its left (Point Ⓐ). The path, easier now, turns right to contour behind The Needle, and across the head of a gully of grass and stones.

It then heads into a narrow gap between two rock towers (Point Ⓑ). The gritty passage between the two towers is slightly awkward, and has an extraordinary atmosphere, like a slot canyon or limestone ravine transported to a Hebridean hillside. Even if the raiders could believe this was the way to the cows – and they wouldn't – a single man could defend it against any number.

The path runs forward through a hollow full of pinnacles and then uphill. When the rock wall of The Table blocks further upward progress, head along its base to the left. Now with the much higher cliff of Meall na Suiramach above you, pass up and to the right, into the gap behind The Table, where you'll find a path to its flat top (Point Ⓒ). It's a perfect picnic spot with room for several thousand people.

Two large rock towers block part of the outward view from The Table. The gap between them has a pencil-shaped pinnacle. This gap is not the way down, but provides the marker for starting the descent. Directly above the pencil pinnacle, a short rocky path drops off the edge of The Table. At the terrace below turn left into a wide gully 50yds (46m) to the left of the pencil pinnacle.

A small path goes down the gully. After 100yds (91m), a tower stands in the gully floor and the path goes down to the right of this. Below the tower it slants steeply down to the left, to join the main Quiraing path, just above a small peat pool (Point Ⓓ). Turn left along Walk 33 for 0.25 mile (400m) to Point ❸.

Skye and the Sea

A comfortable coastal track above Loch Brittle and on to a former fortified peninsula.

DISTANCE 5.25 miles (8.4km) **MINIMUM TIME** 2hrs 15min

ASCENT/GRADIENT 400ft (122m) ▲▲▲ **LEVEL OF DIFFICULTY** ✦✦✦

PATHS *Track, then rough path, 1 stile*

LANDSCAPE *Rocky moorland and coastline*

SUGGESTED MAP *OS Explorer 411 Skye – Cuillin Hills*

START/FINISH *Grid reference: NG 409206*

DOG FRIENDLINESS *On leads*

PARKING *Walkers' pull-off at gate into Glenbrittle campsite*

PUBLIC TOILETS *Glenbrittle campsite*

WALK 35 DIRECTIONS

This is an easy coastal walk on good, firm paths. It's popular on days when the mountains are under a cloak of cloud and hillwalkers don't fancy attempting the famous Inaccessible Pinnacle up on the ridge. But the views back from Creag Mhor make it just as worthwhile, even on those very special days when you can actually see the Cuillin Hills.

From the parking area, the track leads on through the campsite to a kissing gate. The campsite shop, which sells ice cream and midge nets, is just up to the left here. Go through the gate and pass to the left of the campsite's toilet block to cross a stile. Here paths divide; take the right-hand one, below a water tank.

The path runs just above the shoreline and is reasonably clear and firm. After crossing one fair-sized stream, 1 mile (1.6km) out from the camp site it reaches the much larger Allt Coire Lagan, which drains the high wild corrie visited in Walk 32.

If the stream is too full to cross, head upstream for a short distance to a footbridge, then continue up to join a track that runs parallel to the path at a slightly higher level. If you do manage to cross the Allt Coire Lagan, the path continues beyond, becoming gradually fainter and bearing up left to join the track just mentioned.

Across Loch Brittle is a landscape of flat layers, typical basalt country formed from lava flows. You are crossing similar ground

---

WHAT TO LOOK FOR

For those who go adventuring beyond Slochd Dubh, there's a neolithic chambered cairn at the north end of Loch na h-Airde. A wall runs from the sea to the loch head, with a gap for the path – the cairn is just before the wall, and about 20yds (18m) to the left of the gap. Its entrance archway still stands, although its central room has collapsed. Pieces of pottery and six skeletons were found here.

on the walk, very different from the jagged Cuillins above. The track fords a stream on bare rock, with a little gorge and waterfall just above. Now the way, while remaining easy, becomes more exciting; a low outcrop is above, and the top edge of sea cliffs are just below the path. At the next stream crossing, where the track bends slightly down towards the sea, take a path forking up to the left. It ascends gradually, crossing a small stream and reaching the corner of a lochan. This moorland pool, with its bogbean and waterlilies, is a foreground for the Cuillin peaks. From here you're looking straight into Coire Lagan. At the back right corner of the corrie is Sgurr Alasdair, the highest point of Skye.

Just beyond the lochan, the path divides: keep up slightly right, onto the flat-topped rock knoll of Creag Mhor. Continue to a rounded knoll just beyond. Ahead and to the left is the island of Soay. Further away, the Isle of Rum is of the same rugged black rock as the Cuillins.

ago there were still 20 families living here. A small canal has been built to let rowing galleys through at high tide into the small Loch na h-Airde. Above it is a fortified promontory or dun whose stonework still stands. All this ground today is very tough walking, where the small paths peter out into a jumble of bog and crag. Directions for this, if you want them, are simple. Go past the wall that runs along the Slochd Dubh, get lost, then come back to the same point.

Your route goes down to the Slochd Dubh and then turns back. From Creag Mhor the direct descent into the valley is steep, so head left 100yds (91m) then head down a grassy gap with a small path. At the foot of the slope, turn right onto the start of the track. It runs back below the outcrop of Creag Mhor, with the sea below on your left, and soon rejoins the outward route.

Looking down to the right, towards Loch Brittle, you can see the return path just below. Ahead, a faultline valley crosses the entire peninsula from side to side. This is the Slochd Dubh, or Black Gap. For thousands of years, the peninsula beyond the Slochd Dubh was a place of settlement and sanctuary, the stronghold of the MacAskills. Only 150 years

For a slightly easier return to the campsite, keep following the rough track that runs above the path of the outward journey. At the ford of Allt Coire Lagan, go down to the footbridge if necessary, then rejoin the track. Once above the campsite, a small path on the left runs down to the toilet block. Just beyond it, you can bear left to follow the beach back to the car park.

A Raasay Roundabout

*Seaside and woodland lead to Raasay's
old iron-mining railway.*

DISTANCE 7.75 miles (12.5km)	MINIMUM TIME 3hrs 45min	
ASCENT/GRADIENT 820ft (250m) ▲▲▲	LEVEL OF DIFFICULTY ✦✦✦	

PATHS *Small but clear paths, some tracks, 1 stile*

LANDSCAPE *Shingle beaches, woodland and moorland*

SUGGESTED MAP *OS Explorer 409 Raasay, Rona & Scalpay or
410 Skye – Portree & Bracadale*

START/FINISH *Grid reference: NG 555342*

DOG FRIENDLINESS *Close control in woodland and moor, keep on lead
near livestock*

PARKING *Ferry terminal at Sconser, Skye (or lay-by to east)*

PUBLIC TOILETS *Sconser ferry terminal and start of walk*

In his *Journal of a Tour to the Hebrides with Samuel Johnson* (1773), Scottish
biographer James Boswell described the island of Raasay. 'It was a
most pleasing approach to Raasay. We saw before us a beautiful bay, well
defended with a rocky coast; a good gentleman's house, a fine verdure
about it, a considerable number of trees, and beyond it hills and mountains
in gradation of wildness. Our boatmen sung with great spirit.'

Boswell and Macleod

Boswell found Raasay a delight. He enjoyed the company of Macleod the
laird and his ten beautiful daughters, he was impressed by the fine food and
the two pet parrots, he enjoyed the landscape and he very much enjoyed
his walk. He rose before six and, after a light breakfast of dry bread and
whisky, set off with the laird. The aim was the island's highest point, Dun
Caan. Once there, they lunched on cold mutton and brandy, and danced a
Highland reel on its flat summit. They returned by way of Beinn a' Chapuill,
and in the afternoon 'there came a heavy rain, by which we were a great
deal wet'. Their walk totalled 24 miles altogether (39km). By way of a
warm-down, Boswell 'exerted himself extraordinarily in dancing, drinking
porter heavily'.

'If I had my wife and little daughters with me, I would stay long enough,'
said Boswell. And today Raasay, with its well-laid paths (22 of them,
all together), its woodlands and moors and small beaches, offers
walking for everyone, with none of the mainland's turgid bog and skin-
shredding gabbro.

Boswell and his companion Dr Johnson felt highly honoured by the
boatman who ferried them to Raasay, for just 27 years before, the sailor
had carried the Bonnie Prince in the opposite direction. Prince Charles
Stuart had sheltered on Raasay for as long as was safe, then crossed to the
mainland and walked across the moors to Strath. The boatman told Boswell
that the prince had been a stronger walker than himself, but that he'd had to

dissuade him from littering the countryside with his empty brandy bottle. Even today, some walkers need similar education.

As punishment for sheltering the prince, the island was stripped of its cattle and every house burnt. The restoration of Raasay House was almost complete when Boswell visited. He had just one complaint. While the ruins of the former castle boasted an ancient garderobe, the new house had no such 'convenience', and Johnson reproached the laird accordingly. 'You take very good care of one end of a man, but not of the other!'

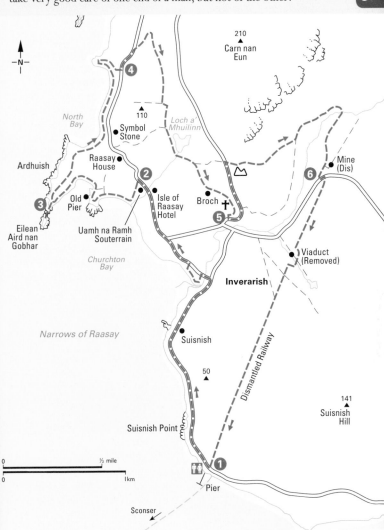

WALK 36 DIRECTIONS

❶ CalMac ferries run roughly hourly during the day to the island of Raasay. Turn left on the island's small road. At Inverarish, turn left over a bridge and divert left past cottages and along the shore. After a playing field you then rejoin the road, which leads past the Isle of Raasay Hotel to another road junction.

WALK 36

② Uamh na Ramh souterrain is over a stile on the left. Continue ahead past the superb but neglected stable block (ahead now is Raasay House, an outdoor centre). At the corner of the stable, turn left, signed 'Clachan'. A track continues below the ramparts of an old gun battery decorated with two stone mermaids. From the pier, follow a path around the bay, until a gate leads to a pleasant shoreline path to Eilean Aird nan Gobhar. Check the tides before crossing the rocks to this tidal island.

③ Head inland over a rock knoll, then pass along the left-hand edge of a plantation on a muddy path overhung by rhododendron. Continue along the shore of North Bay, with a pine plantation on your right, round to a headland. Go up briefly through the low basalt cliff and return along its top. Head along the left edge of the plantation, to emerge through a decorative iron gate on to a road.

④ Turn left for 180yds (165m) to a grey gate on the right. A green track leads up and to the right into a craggy valley. At a walled paddock it turns left and right to join a tarred track. Follow this down past a lily lochan (Loch a' Mhuilinn) and turn left across its dam. Join a wide path running up under larch and rhododendron

but, in 100yds (91m), bear right, waymarked 'Temptation Hill Trail'. Look out for a side path on the right which leads up to Dun Bhorogh Dail, the remains of an Iron Age broch (tower). The main path leads down to pass an austere white church, then bends to the right and drops to a tarred road.

⑤ Turn sharp left up the road for 0.25 mile (400m), then right at a signpost for Burma Road. The track shrinks to a path as it bends left and climbs quite steeply. It becomes a forest track, passing white waymarkers, finally reaching the abandoned buildings of an old iron mine.

⑥ When you get to the tarred road beyond, turn up left to a signpost for the Miners' Trail. Here turn right on the green track of a former railway. Where a viaduct has been removed, a new-built path descends steeply and then climbs again to regain the railbed. The blue-waymarked Miners' Trail turns off, but your route follows the railway onwards, across a stretch of moor and down to the ferry terminal.

Seeing Sea Eagles at Portree Bay

A coastal walk to a raised beach called The Bile,
then returning by way of Ben Chracaig

DISTANCE 3.5 miles (5.7km)   **MINIMUM TIME** 1hr 15min

ASCENT/GRADIENT 459ft (140m) ▲▲▲   **LEVEL OF DIFFICULTY** +++

PATHS Smooth, well-made paths, farm track, 3 stiles

LANDSCAPE Views across Minch from wooded coast and hill above

SUGGESTED MAP OS Explorer 409 Raasay, Rona & Scalpay or
410 Skye – Portree & Bracadale

START Grid reference: NG 485436

DOG FRIENDLINESS Dogs on lead through farmland, scoop poop on shore path

PARKING On A855 (Staffin Road) above Portree Bay. Another small parking
area near slipway

PUBLIC TOILETS Town centre, just off main square

While walking beside Portree Bay, keep at least one eye looking out to sea. You may spot what has been described as Britain's greatest conservation story.

Sea Eagle Story

The last sea eagle in Scotland died on Skye in the early 1900s. Like all large raptors, it was shot at by shepherds and gamekeepers. An attempt to reintroduce them in 1959 failed. In 1975, a secret RAF mission flew four young birds from Norway to the island of Rum. Over the next ten years, they were joined by 80 more. Today, about a dozen pairs are nesting here, with a total population of around 100 spread up along the western coast and the Hebrides.

In Gaelic it is called 'iolaire suil na greine' – the eagle with the sunlit eye – as its eye is a golden colour. In English it's also called the white-tailed eagle, the white-tailed fish eagle and the European sea eagle; it hasn't been back here long enough to finalise its name. Its nickname is the 'flying barn door' because it's so big, but it's not a heavy bird. Even with its 8ft (2.4m) wingspan, it weighs in at just 7lb (3kg). The sea eagle nests in cliffs. One nest, with an RSPB hide, is at Loch Frisa on Mull, another here at Portree. The Aros Experience visitor centre has a closed-circuit TV camera trained on the nest, and the Portree fishermen have taken to throwing seafood to the birds outside the bay. The eagle feeds by snatching fish out of the sea – but even more spectacular is its mating display, when the two birds soar and cartwheel high above the water.

Was that an Eagle?

The first few eagles you think you see are almost certainly buzzards. When you see a real eagle, and even though you can't tell how far away it is, you'll know it for what it is. It's four times the size of a buzzard and its wingbeats are so slow and powerful. That's when it isn't gliding from one horizon to

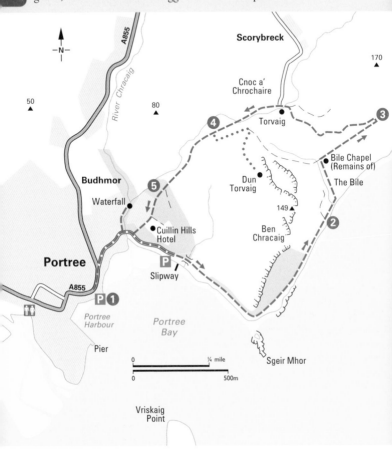
the other apparently without moving a feather. The sea eagle is even bigger than the golden one, and has a white tail – but so does a young golden eagle. But if the eagle is flying over the sea, and especially if it's over the sea at Portree, then it's a sea eagle.

Naturalists believed that the bird's main problem would be the golden eagle, which during the years of extinction had taken over the nest sites. But sadly, the real enemy is still humans. In 2000, and despite a 24-hour guard, thieves took the two eggs from the Mull pair.

WALK 37 DIRECTIONS

1 Turn off the main A855 on to a lane signed 'Budh Mor', to walk down to the shoreline and then continue to a small parking area. A tarred path continues along the shore past a slipway. After a footbridge, it passes under hazels which show the typical ground-branching habit of bushes formerly coppiced, cut back every

seven years for firewood. The path passes below a viewpoint with flagpoles and then rounds the headland to reach the edge of a level green field called The Bile.

2 A wall runs up the edge of The Bile. A sign points up left for Scorybreck but ignore it and go through a small gate ahead. A rough path leads into the corner of The Bile field. Go up its left edge and turn across its top, to a stile just above a field gate. Cross the top of the next field on an old green path, to a stile at its corner. You will see a track just beyond.

3 Turn sharp left, up the track. At the top it passes through two gates to reach a stony road just to the right of Torvaig. Turn left past the house and cross the foot of a tarred road into a gently descending track. It runs down between two large corrugated sheds and then through to a gate with a stile.

> ### WHILE YOU'RE THERE
> The Aros Experience, just south of Portree, has the RSPB's closed-circuit TV link with the sea eagle nest. Nest action is between April and July (the young hatch in April). The centre also has an exhibition and audio-visual centre dedicated to the people of Skye, including Bonnie Prince Charlie. Outside there are some short forest walks.

> ### WHERE TO EAT AND DRINK
> There is a wide choice of pubs and cafés above the harbour. On the pier itself is the Lower Deck seafood restaurant, with a chip shop for those in a hurry. Vegetarians should head for Café Arriba. For an unpretentious pub meal try the Tongadale Hotel.

4 The grassy path ahead leads down into Portree, but you can take a short, rather rough, diversion to Dun Torvaig (an ancient fortified hilltop) above. For the dun, turn left along the fence, and left again on a well-made path above. It leads to a kissing gate above the two sheds. Turn sharp right along the fence for a few steps, then bear left around the base of a small outcrop and head straight up on a tiny path

> ### WHAT TO LOOK OUT FOR
> The strangely level meadow called The Bile is a raised beach that formed during the ice age. As the ice melted, the sea level rose, but at the same time, the land rose much further as the weight of overlying ice was removed. The result is that this former beach is now 100ft (30m) above the sea.

to the dun. Remnants of dry-stone walling can be seen around the summit. Return to the well-made path, passing above Point **4** to join the wall on the right. The path leads down under goat willows into a wood where it splits; stay close to the wall.

5 At the first houses (The Parks Bungalow 5), keep downhill on a tarred street. On the left is the entrance to the Cuillin Hills Hotel. A few steps later, fork right on to a stony path. At the shore road, turn right across a stream and at once right again on a path that runs up for 60yds (55m) to a craggy little waterfall. Return to the shore road and turn right to the walk start.

Waterstein Head

*Through crofting country and peat moors
to a 1,000ft (305m) sea cliff.*

DISTANCE 5.75 miles (9.2km)   MINIMUM TIME 3hrs 30min

ASCENT/GRADIENT 1,500ft (457m) ▲▲▲   LEVEL OF DIFFICULTY ✦✦✦

PATHS Grassy clifftops and moorland, 2 fences and 1 gate

LANDSCAPE Cliff tops high above Atlantic Ocean

SUGGESTED MAP OS Explorer 407 Skye – Dunvegan

START/FINISH Grid reference: NG 163443

DOG FRIENDLINESS On short lead – risk of scaring sheep over cliff edges

PARKING Ramasaig road end or pull-ins at pass 0.75 mile (1.2km) north

PUBLIC TOILETS Glendale village hall

After the defeat of Bonnie Prince Charlie's uprising in 1746, the clan system was swept away. But the clansmen were still there, transformed into crofters. Elsewhere, such subsistence smallholders go by the honourable name of 'peasant farmers', with 25 acres (10ha), a kailyard, a cow and some sheep on the hill.

Rents rose, partly to support the landlords' new London lifestyles. Crofting lands were cleared to make way for sheep, and the crofters were forced to relocate, first to the shore and later right out of the country to Canada and Australia. By the late 1800s, they were starting to fight back. In 1882, crofters at the Braes, south of Portree, resisted an eviction. Fifty Glasgow policemen were sent to restore order, and in the 'Battle of the Braes' the crofters retaliated with sticks and stones.

In Glendale, land-starved crofters deliberately let their cattle stray onto neighbouring farms. Government forces and the gunboat Jackal were defied by 600 crofters. There were four arrests, including John Macpherson, the 'Glendale Martyr', and a minister, the Reverend D MacCallum. The 'martyrs' received two-month prison sentences. The public outcry that followed saw a newly formed 'Crofters' Party' – distant forerunner of today's New Labour – send four MPs to Westminster. The first of the Crofting Acts, passed by Gladstone's government, led to less unfair rents and security of tenure.

Today, thanks to those battles of long ago, Glendale and the Braes are inhabited lands where so much of Scotland is bleak and empty. Crofters now have the right to buy and enjoy subsidies and grants from the government. Few crofts provide enough to live on, without a part-time job on the side. As a result there's a series of small-scale, off-beat and interesting tourist enterprises along the Glendale Visitor Route.

Peat became the crofters' fuel supply and in a few places it is still being worked today. Above Loch Eishort on this walk you'll see the little triangular stacks, each made from four peats, drying in the wind (and of course getting wet again in the rain). And when it burns, it brings the smell of the wild bog-moss right into the house.

RAMASAIG

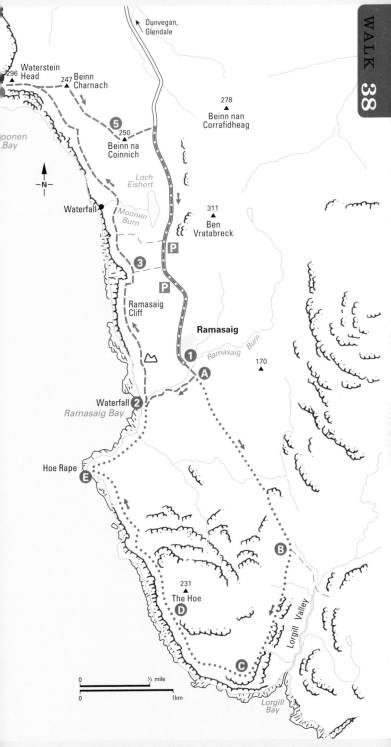

Dunvegan,
Glendale

Waterstein
Head
296

247 Beinn
Charnach

Moonen
Bay

5 250
Beinn na
Coinnich

278
Beinn nan
Corrafidheag

Loch
Eishort

Moonen
Burn

Waterfall

311
Ben
Vratabreck

P

3

P

Ramasaig
Cliff

Ramasaig

1

170

A

Ramasaig Burn

Waterfall 2
Ramasaig Bay

B

Hoe Rape E

231
The Hoe

D

C

Lorgill Valley

0   ½ mile
0   1km

Lorgill
Bay

WALK 38 DIRECTIONS

① From the end of the tarmac, the road continues as a track past farm buildings, with a bridge over the Ramasaig Burn. After a gate it reaches a shed with a tin roof. Bear right and follow the left bank of Ramasaig Burn to the shore.

② Cross the burn at a ford and head up a very steep meadow beside the fence that protects the cliff edge. There's a rather awkward fence to cross half-way up. At the top, above Ramasaig Cliff, keep following the fence on the left. It cuts across to the right to protect a notch in the cliff edge. From here, you could cut down to the parking areas at the nearby road pass.

③ Keep downhill along the cliffside fence. At the bottom, a turf wall off to the right provides

another short-cut back to the road. The clifftop walk now bears slightly right around the V-notch of the Moonen Burn. A small path crosses the stream and slants up left to rejoin the clifftop fence, which soon turns slightly inland around another cliff notch. The cliff-edge fence leads up and to the left, to reach Waterstein Head. Here there is a trig point, 971ft (296m) above the sea – the second highest cliff on Skye. Below, you will see Neist Point lighthouse.

④ Return for 0.25 mile (400m) down to where the fence bends to the right, then continue through a shallow grassy col for the slight rise to Beinn Charnach. Here bear right to follow a gently rounded grass ridge-line parallel with cliffs. The highest line along the ridge is the driest. A fence runs across, with a grey gate at its highest point where it passes through a col. Climb over the gate and on up to a cairn on Beinn na Coinnich.

⑤ Continue along the slightly rocky plateau for 300yds (274m) to the south-east top. Now the Ramasaig road is visible 0.25 mile (400m) away on the left. Go down to join a quad-bike track heading towards the road. Just before reaching the road, the bike track crosses a swampy col. This shows old and recent peat workings. Turn right, along the road, passing above Loch Eishort to the start.

High Cliffs at Hoe Rape

An abandoned valley leads to black sea cliffs above the Atlantic.
See map and information panel for Walk 38

DISTANCE *5.25 miles (8.4km)*   MINIMUM TIME *3hrs 15min*

ASCENT/GRADIENT *900ft (274m)* ▲▲▲   LEVEL OF DIFFICULTY +++

WALK 39 DIRECTIONS (Walk 38 option)

From the road end (Point **1**), head down the track between farm buildings and across Ramasaig Burn to a stone shed with a tin roof – a former black house (Point **A**). This is where Walk 38 turns right, but continue slightly left on the main track. At the next right-hand bend of the track, the hummocks of former lazybed cultivation are above on the left. The track crosses a ford and climbs over moorland, descending to a gate (Point **B**), with a view into Lorgill Valley.

Don't go through the gate but turn right on a trace of path. The way now follows the top of the steep ground, with the Lorgill Valley below on the left. This former settlement has just one building remaining, another former black house, re-roofed in slate. Old field enclosures and lazybeds can be clearly seen. Behind, the moor rises in terraces and long, low outcrops – typical lava landscape (see Walk 33).

Follow the top edge of one such outcrop, then a grassed-over old wall. Where this wall line appears to vanish, go up a few steps to find it again above a trickle waterfall. Eventually the wall heads off up to the right, away from the drop to Lorgill. Keep ahead, climbing a little, sticking to the valley rim. Follow the top of a line of outcrops round the point above Lorgill Bay (Point **C**). Look back along the coast to see the tall sea-stacks called Macleod's Maidens, visible only from this one point on the walk.

The way is now clear, keeping to the short grass near the edge of tremendous cliffs on the left. The ground rises gently, soon following iron posts of an old fence. You cross an old wall (Point **D**), and in 0.25 mile (400m) the ground starts to drop. A fence running across guards a large notch in the cliff edge, keep round to its right. With the cliffs now much lower, you could head out left on to the grassy promontory of Hoe Rape (Point **E**).

Continue along the shoreline, around Ramasaig Bay, crossing more lazybed hummocks. Cross a stream to a field gate – climbing over this locked gate is easier than crossing the fence later on. Either way, turn left along the fence to the Ramasaig Burn (Point **2**). The stream plunges to the beach in a waterfall, which was seen from Hoe Rape, but isn't visible from above. Turn up alongside the stream to the farm buildings at Ramasaig – or cross the burn to continue with Walk 38.

The Shores of Loch Shieldaig

WALK 40

A walk around the many inlets of the Shieldaig peninsula.

DISTANCE 3.25 miles (5.3km)   **MINIMUM TIME** 1hr 45min

ASCENT/GRADIENT 500ft (152m) ▲▲▲   **LEVEL OF DIFFICULTY** ✦✦✦

PATHS Well-made old paths, 1 rough section

LANDSCAPE Saltwater views up Loch Torridon and down Loch Shieldaig

SUGGESTED MAP OS Explorer 428 Kyle of Lochalsh

START/FINISH Grid reference: NG 814538

DOG FRIENDLINESS Keep on lead in village and when passing livestock

PARKING South end of Shieldaig village, opposite shop and hotel

PUBLIC TOILETS North end of village (another car park)

WALK 40 DIRECTIONS

A hundred years ago, all you needed to connect your cottage to civilisation was a well-made path to keep your feet dry. Today, a powerboat to the nearby pier is the preferred way to visit the neighbours and bring the shopping home. However, the paths to two cottages north of Shieldaig village are still there to be walked; a single path at first, that divides at the base of Shieldaig promontory to form a Y-shape. No historic path links the two top points of the Y, so for this short section of the walk the going is rather rougher.

Place names ending in 'aig' (the equivalent of the Norse 'vik') are Norse harbours. So Shieldaig (Shill Vik) is Herring Harbour. Follow the street along the shoreline past a cannon salvaged from the Spanish Armada of 1588. At the village end it rises slightly, with another parking area, and a war memorial above on the right.

In front of the village school, turn right up a rough track. The track passes a couple of houses to turn left. In another 100yds (91m) it divides; here the main track for Rubha Lodge forks off left, but your route bears right, passing to the right of a glacier-smoothed rock knoll.

Offshore, densely wooded Shieldaig Island shows how rich the natural vegetation would be without grazing deer and sheep. All over the Highlands, projects to fence off some of the lower slopes are aiming to re-create tree-clad scenes of 2,000 years ago. It isn't even necessary to replant

WHILE YOU'RE THERE

The natural tree cover of the Highlands is pine, oak or birch, depending on the local climate. Ancient ashwood is a surprise. Rassal ashwood grows on a small outcrop of limestone, and pollen in peat sediments suggests that it's 6,000 years old. Now fenced as a National Nature Reserve, it is regrowing its original limestone-loving wild flowers. The reserve's small car park is on the single-track A896 at Grid ref: NG 840432.

as pockets of remaining forest and trees on crags away from the nibblers spread seed naturally into the protected areas.

The terraced path runs through birch woods at first, with Loch Shieldaig below on the left. It passes above two rocky bays, then strikes across a peat bog, bright in mid-summer with bell heather and the fluffy white tops of cotton grass. In the middle of this flat area it divides at a cairn.

The right-hand path runs along the edge of the peaty area, with rocky ground above on its left, then next to birch trees for 50yds (46m). Look out for the point where its pink gravel surface becomes peaty, with a rock formation like a low ruin on the right, because here is an easily missed path junction.

What seems like the main footpath, ahead and slightly downhill, peters out eventually. The correct path forks off to the left, slanting up to the higher ground just above. The path is now clear, crossing slabby ground in the direction of the peninsula's trig point, 0.25 mile (400m) away. After 220yds (201m) it rises

slightly to a gateway in a former fence. Aiming right of the trig point, it crosses a small heather moor. At a broken wall, the path turns down right through a gap to the top of a grassy meadow. The first of the two shoreline cottages, Bad-callda, is just below. Rough paths lead to the left across the boggy top of the meadow and above a birchwood, with the trig point just above on the left. Keep going forward at the same level to a heather knoll, with a pole on it. Just below you is a second cottage, called Camas-ruadh.

The footpath zig-zags down to the right between rocks. White paint spots lead round to the right of the cottage and its shed. Turn left behind the shed to join a clear path coming from the cottage.

The return path is nice and easy to follow, mostly along the top of the slope dropping to the right to Loch Shieldaig. After 0.5 mile (800m) it rejoins the outward route at the cairn.

Overleaf: Green hills and countryside surround the shores of Loch Sheildaig (Walk 40)

Coire Lair and the Coulin Forest

*Deer stalkers' paths lead into the heart of the
South Torridon mountains.*

DISTANCE 9 miles (14.5km) MINIMUM TIME 5hrs

ASCENT/GRADIENT 1,700ft (518m) ▲▲▲ LEVEL OF DIFFICULTY ✦✦✦

PATHS Well-made path, then track, no stiles

LANDSCAPE Boulder-scattered moorland between high hills

SUGGESTED MAP OS Explorer 429 Glen Carron & West Monar

START/FINISH Grid reference: NH 005484

DOG FRIENDLINESS Keep under control in deer forest

PARKING On A890 below Achnashellach Station

PUBLIC TOILETS None en route

NOTE During stalking season on Achnashellach Estate (15 September–
20 October, not Sundays), keep strictly to route, which is right of way

The path winds up from Strath Carron into Coire Lair. The corrie is a
fine one, with scattered pines, waterfalls and craggy mountains. The
path that takes you there is terraced at the steep places, drained at the
level places and avoids the boggy places altogether. Over a century old, it
was built not for walkers but stalkers – or rather for their sturdy Highland
ponies bringing down a deer corpse weighing 2cwt (100kg) or more.
Recent resurfacing has been done sympathetically in the traditional style.

Deer stalking calls on the legs and the intelligence in equal measure,
appealing to man's ancient hunting urges. 'The beautiful motions of the
deer, his sagacity and the skilful generalship that can alone ensure success
in the pursuit of him, keep the mind in a pleasurable state of constant
excitement.' Thus said William Scrope Esq, in the book *Days of Deerstalking*,
which presented this sport to the leisured and affluent of 1845.

Red Bedrock

As the path rises above the tree line, you'll notice slabs of Torridonian
sandstone underfoot – the ghillies have deliberately routed it over this
maintenance-free surface. On the left, Fuar Tholl ('cold hole') is of the
same red rock, but ahead on the right, Beinn Liath Mhor is composed of
pale Cambrian quartzite. As you top the pass and look east, the hills ahead
are rounded, grey and slightly less exciting all the way to the North Sea.
As you come to know Scotland you realise that all the way along its north-
western edge there's a zone of rather special hills. Applecross, Torridon, the
Great Wilderness, Coigach, Inverpolly: these names mean sandstone and
quartzite to the geologist, and pure magic to the mountaineer.

The rest of the Northern Highlands is made of a speckly grey rock
–Moinian schist. The boundary line is the Moine Thrust. It's called a
'thrust' because these grey mountains have been pushed in over the top of
the Torridonian red and the Cambrian white. It marks the western limit of
the crumple zone from when England crashed into Scotland 400 million

years ago. On the face of Beinn Liath Mhor, the arrival of the Moinian has crumpled the quartzite, like a boot landing on a carelessly placed cheese sandwich. A short wander from Point ❸ further into the corrie will show this more clearly, and you'll also see the famous Mainreachan Buttress on the north side of Fuar Tholl.

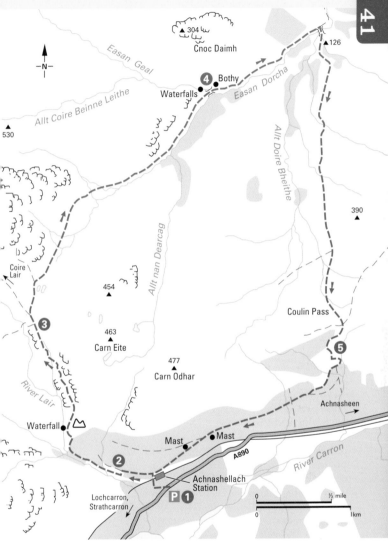

WALK 41 DIRECTIONS

❶ The track to the station runs up behind a red phone box, then turns right to reach the platform end. Cross the line through two gates and head up the stony track opposite, past a waymarker arrow.

After 100yds (91m) you reach a junction under low-voltage power lines. Turn left here on a smooth gravel road to a gate through a deer fence. After 0.25 mile (400m), look out for a signpost where a new path turns back to the left.

2 This path goes back through the deer fence, then runs up alongside the River Lair. As the slope steepens above the tree-line, a short side path on the left gives a view of a waterfall. The well-maintained stalkers' path runs over slabs of bare sandstone. A cairn marks the point where it arrives in the upper valley, Coire Lair, with a view to the high pass at its head, 2 miles (3.2km) away.

3 About 200yds (183m) after this first cairn, another marks a junction of paths. Bear right here, between two pools. In 110yds (100m) there is a second junction with a tall, well-built cairn. Bear right, on a path that leaves the corrie through a wide, shallow col just 350yds (320m) above. An elegant conical cairn marks a final path junction. Bear right; in a few steps you're heading downhill above the path. The path runs downhill among drumlins and sandstone boulders, slanting down to the right to join the wooded Allt nan Dearcag. The path now runs down alongside this stream; you may notice pale grey quartzite. The path drops to reach a footbridge. This bridge crosses a side stream, the Allt Coire Beinne Leithe, with the Easan Geal, White Waterfalls, just above.

4 At an open bothy shelter hut, a track continues downhill, with the gorge of the Easan Dorcha (Dark Waterfalls) on its right.

After a mile (1.6km) there's a stone bridge on the right. Turn across this, on to a track that runs up the wide, open valley to the Coulin Pass at its head. Coulin, pronounced Cowlinn, is the name of the deer forest, the river and the loch at its foot. Gaelic 'Cuilion' means holly tree.

5 After the pass, the track goes through a gate into plantations, then bends right to slant down the side of Strath Carron. At a Scottish Rights of Way Society signpost, follow the main track ahead towards Achnashellach. A clear-felled area gives views to the left, then the trees are bigger until just before you cross a bridge to a mobile phone mast. Fork left, just before a second mast, and descend gently to reach the junction above Achnashellach Station.

Following the Diabaig Coast Path

A walk above Loch Torridon in the footsteps of the fairy folk – the legendary Duine Sithe.

DISTANCE 9.5 miles (15.3km)	**MINIMUM TIME** 6hrs
ASCENT/GRADIENT 1,805ft (550m) ▲▲▲	**LEVEL OF DIFFICULTY** +++

PATHS Narrow, rough and wet in places, no stiles

LANDSCAPE Rocky knolls and small lochans

SUGGESTED MAP OS Explorer 433 Torridon – Beinn Eighe & Liathach

START/FINISH Grid reference: NG 842073

DOG FRIENDLINESS Keep on lead passing Alligin Shuas and near sheep

PARKING Wester Alligin, pull-in on side road near Alligin River

PUBLIC TOILETS Torridon village

New Year's Eve in Wester Ross is a time when old songs are sung, whisky is drunk (not all of it approved by the exciseman either) and tales are told in both English and Gaelic. Over the years these stories mature and grow, and also change location, so that the tailor who lost his hump to the fairies lived not only in Scotland, but in Ireland and even Italy.

Fairy Tales and Ghosts

Many of the tales told in Alligin take place in the knolly, magical ground on the way to Diabaig. One story concerns two villagers who were bringing whisky for the New Year from Gairloch by way of the coast path. They heard wonderful music and came upon a cave in the hill where the fairy people had started their Hogmanay celebrations a few hours early. Fascinated, the man with the keg crept closer and closer until he was actually inside, whereupon the cave closed up and disappeared. A year later the other man came back, found the cave open and dragged his friend out across the threshold. The friend thought he'd been in there only a few minutes, but of the whisky he carried there was no trace.

At the top of the hill road is tiny Lochan Dearg, and here there is a ghost that appears only to people bearing his own name, Murdo Mackenzie. The kilted spirit, one of the Mackenzies of Gairloch, was slain by a Torridon MacDonald and buried somewhere near by.

Horse Tales and Fairy Folk

Loch Diabaigas Airde (Point ③) is haunted by the water spirit called the kelpie. This appears as a magnificent white horse, but if you mount it, the horse gallops rapidly into the loch and you're never seen again. That is, unless you just happen to have a bridle that's made of pure silver to tame it. Another kelpie lives in the Lochan Toll nam Biast, the Lochan of the Beast Hole, at the back of Beinn Alligin.

Fairy music has been heard above the gorge of the Alligin burn. So, to protect yourself from the Duine Sithe, be polite, but don't accept food from them. At best it'll be cow dung, at worst it'll enslave you for ever.

121

LOCH TORRIDON

Carry iron, oatmeal or a groundsel root for protection, and a cry of 'am monadh oirbh, a' bheistein' ('back to the hill, you wee beastie') is effective. Approaching Alligin Shuas, walk carefully past Cnoc nan Sithe, the Fairy Knoll, so as not to disturb them.

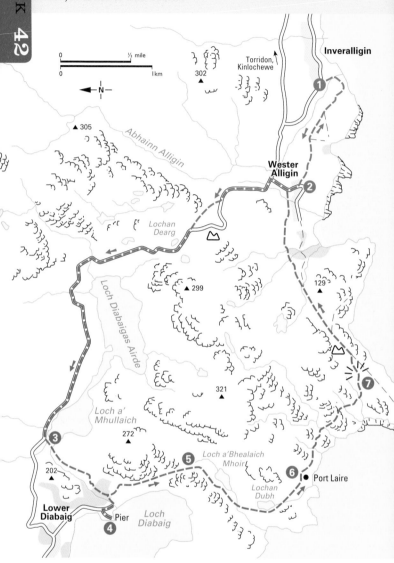

WALK 42 DIRECTIONS

❶ From the parking place, follow the road over the Abhainn Alligin river. A path leads along the shoreline for 100yds (91m) and then makes its way up right among sandstone outcrops. Bear left underneath a power line to join the corner of a tarmac driveway. Keep ahead to reach Wester Alligin.

❷ Turn up the road and then left, on the road for Diabaig. As the road steepens, you can take a

LOCH TORRIDON

path to the right of power lines, rejoining the road across a high pass and then down past two lochs – Loch Diabaigas Airde and Loch a'Mhullaich – which are linked.

❸ Turn off left, crossing the outflow of Loch a'Mhullaich on a footbridge. A clear path leads out along the high wall of a stream valley, then zig-zags down to a grey gate. Go down through woods to a white house, No 1 Diabaig. Turn right to reach the old stone pier.

> **WHILE YOU'RE THERE**
> The National Trust for Scotland has a countryside centre at Torridon village, right below the frowning sandstone wall of Liathach (open April–September). It has audio-visual displays on the scenery and wildlife, with an unstaffed deer museum close by.

❹ Return up the path you just came down to pass a stone shed. Here a sign indicates a turn to the right, under an outcrop and between boulders. The path heads up to a small rock step with an arrow mark and a convenient tree root which you can use to hold on to. It then leads up to a gate in a fence and zig-zags into an open gully with a large crag on the right. At the top of this, it turns right along a shelf, with still more crag above. The path slants gently down along the foot of another crag, then up to a col.

> **WHERE TO EAT AND DRINK**
> Mrs Ross at Ben Bhraggie in Diabaig sometimes offers teas. Look for the notice outside the house. But carry food, as the next shop is at Torridon village.

❺ From here the path is small but clear. It bends right to Loch

> **WHAT TO LOOK OUT FOR**
> You'll pass grey Lewisian gneiss, worn into knolly shapes by glaciers. Look closely and you'll see it has coloured zig-zag stripes, like tweed. It is the oldest rock in Britain and is made of other, even older, rocks, bashed about through half the history of the planet.

WALK 42

a'Bhealaich Mhoir and then turns left below it to Lochan Dubh. Cross its outbound flow and slant down left towards the cottage of Port Laire.

❻ Pass above the house, then slant gradually up away from the sea. The path crosses the head of a bracken valley with a ruined croft house into a bleak knolly area out of sight of the sea. Cross two branches of a stream and go up to a cairn which marks where the path bears left up the spur. It now contours across a heathery meadow among the knolls, at the end of which it climbs pink rocks over a final spur. Just ahead is a gate in the deer fence.

❼ The path leads along a level shelf with views to Liathach and the head of Loch Torridon, then it crosses a high, steep slope of heather. Near the end of this slope, the path forks. Take the upper branch, to go through a wide col. The rather boggy path heads down towards Wester Alligin. From a gate above the village, a faint path runs down in the direction of a distant green shed. It descends through a wood, then contours just above the village to reach the road above Point ❷. Retrace your steps to the start of the walk.

WALK 43

Flowerdale Falls

Porpoise-watching along the Gairloch shore,
then up a rocky valley.

DISTANCE 5.25 miles (8.4km)   MINIMUM TIME 2hrs 45min

ASCENT/GRADIENT 800ft (244m) ▲▲▲   LEVEL OF DIFFICULTY +++

PATHS Tracks and smooth paths, mostly waymarked, no stiles

LANDSCAPE Gentle river valley and rocky coast

SUGGESTED MAP OS Explorer 433 Torridon – Beinn Eighe & Liathach
or 434 Gairloch & Loch Ewet

START/FINISH Grid reference: NG 807756 on OS Explorer 433

DOG FRIENDLINESS Keep on lead past Flowerdale House (as signs indicate)

PARKING Beach car park, southern end of Gairloch

PUBLIC TOILETS Walk start and Charlestown pier

On a calm day in 1809, three fisherman drowned in Loch Ewe when their small boat was attacked and sunk by a whale. These waters are among the best in Europe for cetaceans (whales, dolphins and porpoises). The Gulf Stream brings warm, plankton-rich water and the swirling currents around the islands bring nutrients to the surface. The plankton flourish; the fish eat the plankton; the whales and dolphins eat the fish.

Porpoise or Dolphin?

The strongest currents are at headlands and narrow sea passages, so these are good places to look for marine wildlife. Calm days are best, and early morning best of all when looking west, as the low sunlight shines off their wet backs. On most summer days, either the harbour porpoise or common dolphin – or possibly both – can be seen, given a little patience, in Loch Gairloch. But which is which? At 6ft (2m) or less, the porpoise is smaller. It has a short, stubby fin compared with the dolphin's more elegant one. Harbour porpoises are normally shy, but the ones at Gairloch are untypically friendly, often approaching boats. Endangered in the world as a whole, the ones at Gairloch are doing well and a Special Area of Conservation has been proposed for them here.

What the Future Holds

The whaling industry in Scotland ended in 1951, but serious threats remain. Dolphins and porpoises are accidentally caught in fishing nets, and floating plastic rope and old nets are another danger. Pollution from agriculture and forestry releases heavy metals and pesticides into the ocean. Fish farming is also probably damaging the dolphins. More fish sewage than human sewage goes into the Hebridean seas, all of it untreated, and anti-fouling paint on fish farms contributes more chemicals.

Cetaceans use sound signals for finding fish, as well as for communication. Interference comes from ships, dredging nets, seismic oil exploration and underwater beepers fitted to fish farms to keep seals away.

GAIRLOCH

We don't know how well the dolphins and porpoises are doing. The growth of the whale-spotting industry means that we are just starting to discover how the populations are growing or declining. Marine tourism in Scotland today is a booming trade, supporting several hundred jobs. By going on one of these trips, you'll contribute to crucial research. A responsible boatman will not pursue the animals or steer into the middle of a group, but move quietly and wait for the dolphins to approach the boat.

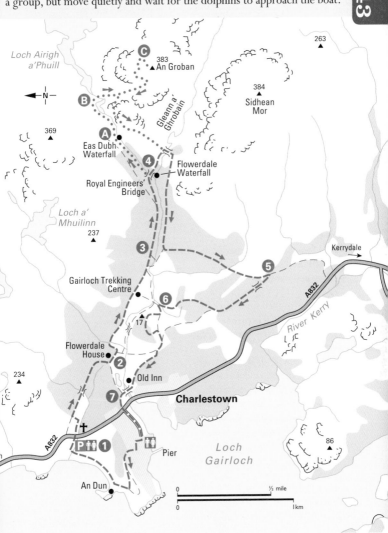

WALK 43 DIRECTIONS

❶ Cross the road and head up to the right of the newer cemetery. Turn left at its corner, going into trees to a path above. Turn right until a footbridge leads on to a wide path that soon runs downhill. The main path bends right (green-top waymarker) and runs down to a tarred driveway.

❷ Turn left along a tarred track to pass Flowerdale House. The

WALK 43

track passes to the left of a lovely old barn and turns right at a sign for the waterfall to pass Gairloch Trekking Centre. In about 0.25 mile (400m) you pass a timber-surfaced bridge on the right.

3 Follow the main path ahead, still to the left of the stream, to reach a footbridge built by the Royal Engineers, just before you get to Flowerdale Waterfall.

4 The path leads up past the waterfall to cross a footbridge above. It runs up into a wind-blown pine clump, then turns back down the valley. After another footbridge it joins a rough track. You pass a memorial to the blind piper of Gairloch, just before a forest road beside Point **3**. Turn left, away from the timber-surfaced bridge, through felled forest that's regenerating naturally (with birch, alder, pine, willow and rowan).

5 A blue-topped pole marks a path to the right with a footbridge. It leads through scrub birch and bracken with blue waymarker poles. The path bends right at an old fence cornerpost and goes down through bracken and birch to pass above and to the left of an enclosed field. Turn right underneath two large oak trees and cross a small stream to an earth track.

6 Turn left for a few steps, until a small bracken path runs up to the right past a waymarked power pole. The path bends left under oaks, then drops to rejoin the earth track. This soon meets a larger track, which is the old road from Loch Maree to Gairloch. Turn right along this, through a couple of gates, to reach the Old Inn at Charlestown.

7 Cross the old bridge, and the main road, towards the pier. Turn right at the signpost for the beach, to a stepped path to the left of Gairloch Chandlery. The tarred path passes to the left of a pinewood, then turns right into the trees. It bends left and emerges to run along the spine of a small headland. Just before being carried out to sea it turns sharp right, and crosses above a rocky bay to the fort (An Dun). A duckboard path runs along the back of the beach, then turns right to the car park.

A Gneiss Little Hill

*A tough ascent following a stream past a waterfall,
and on to a wild and rocky mountain.*
See map and information panel for Walk 43

DISTANCE 7 miles (11.3km)	MINIMUM TIME 4hrs 30min
ASCENT/GRADIENT 1,800ft (548m) ▲▲▲	LEVEL OF DIFFICULTY +++

WALK 44 DIRECTIONS
(Walk 43 option)

The Lewisian gneiss forms a worn and wild landscape, all bare rock, bog and little pools. An Groban is a hill that's as rugged and romantic as a full mountain. This side-trip to reach it starts at Point ❹, just before the Royal Engineers' footbridge. Turn left up the side stream on a small path. After a few steps it bears up left into woods above the stream – this part is steep, narrow and slippery. It regains the riverbank above the Easan Bana (White Waterfall). Keep on up to the left of the stream, to a deer fence (Point ❹).

Fenced areas are great for regenerating birch and pine, but can be a nuisance for walkers. Flowerdale Estate has not only provided a ladder stile on this informal path, but also put very basic stiles all along their fencing. Above the ladder stile, head up to the left of the braided rapids of the upper waterfall (Eas Dubh, the Black Waterfall). Old metal fence posts show the way over rough ground to the left of a small pool with lilies. Cross the stream (Point ❸) before a larger lochan, and eye up the rocky cone of An Groban ahead.

The ascent will be a set of zig-zags on grassy shelves. Once over the stream you'll cross (or briefly use)

a small path marked with posts. Later on, this path will be the descent route. After crossing it, head into a grassy valley that slants up to the right, just below the main rocky pyramid. Follow this valley to the small col at its top. From here you can look across the small Gleann a'Ghrobain to a similar small rocky mountain opposite, Sidhean Mor.

Turn up left, into an open grassy gully with a large cairn in its foot. Go up for 100yds (91m) to a red sandstone boulder in the middle of the little valley. Just above this, a small path heads up to the right. This leads up to a small col, with a perched sandstone boulder up on the left. Here the tiny path turns right for the last 90yds (82m) to the summit (Point ❸), which has a stone trig point.

Going back, you'll use the same route down An Groban's rocky cone and the grassy valley below. Just before the stream, you'll meet the small path with wooden waymarker posts. Turn left along it. It gradually contours out left, away from the stream and around the base of An Groban. In the valley Gleann a' Ghrobain, the path runs down to a ladder stile and joins the broad path of Walk 43 near the Flowerdale burn. Turn left over the footbridge, continuing on Walk 43.

Beinn Eighe Mountain Trail

The toughest waymarked trail in Scotland, to a lunar landscape.

WALK

45

> **DISTANCE** 3.5 miles (5.7km)   **MINIMUM TIME** 2hrs 45min
>
> **ASCENT/GRADIENT** 1,847ft (563m) ▲▲▲   **LEVEL OF DIFFICULTY** +++
>
> **PATHS** Steep well-made path, no stiles
>
> **LANDSCAPE** Pine forest below, bare rock and stones above
>
> **SUGGESTED MAP** OS Explorer 433 Torridon – Beinn Eighe & Liathach
>
> **START/FINISH** Grid reference: NH 002650
>
> **DOG FRIENDLINESS** Permitted only if under close control
>
> **PARKING** Nature trail car park at Coille na Glas-leitire
>
> **PUBLIC TOILETS** Beinn Eighe Visitor Centre, 1.5 miles (2.4km) south, and at Kinlochewe

WALK 45 DIRECTIONS

Beinn Eighe is Britain's oldest National Nature Reserve (1951) and the Mountain Trail is possibly Scotland's toughest nature trail. The route is well waymarked. From the end of the car park, turn left to pass under the road; immediately turn left again, following a sign for the Mountain Trail. The path goes under birches, with a stream on its right, then under pines. It then climbs slightly more steeply, across slabs of reddish sandstone, to the marker cairn named 'Pines'.

Scots pines once clothed all the valley sides of Wester Ross. The ones around Loch Maree were fed into the fires of an iron works directly opposite and the furnaces at Bonawe near Oban.

WHAT TO LOOK FOR

From the top of the trail there's a chance of seeing a golden eagle soaring in thermals of rising air.

More recently, ancient pines were felled to make ammunition boxes during World War Two. Genetic analysis has shown that the pines here are related to those of France and Spain, whereas those in the Cairngorms and eastern Scotland spread after the ice age from northern Europe.

The path climbs more steeply up rough stone steps to a footbridge, and then up more steps with the stream on its right. In the path and under the small waterfalls, you'll see that the bedrock has changed from rounded red sandstone to angular pale-grey quartzite. From the cairn called 'Geology' you can see all three of the distinctive rocks of Wester Ross. Quartzite is underfoot and over-head. Across Loch Maree, the steep-sided stack of Slioch is Torridonian sandstone, standing on a base of greyish Lewisian gneiss. Slioch is a remnant of a thick layer of sandstone laid by flash floods and outwash streams out of a now-vanished mountain range; the gneiss surface now uncovered represents a landscape that first felt the air 500 million years ago.

The gneiss and sandstone date from long before multi-celled life on earth. The younger quartzite on top shows some of the oldest fossils and at the cairn called 'Trumpet Rock' you can see some of them. These are the trumpet-shaped entrances of worm-holes, made when the rock was still sea-bottom sludge.

WHERE TO EAT AND DRINK

The Kinlochewe Hotel serves good home-cooked food and innumerable whiskies, as well as a beer named after Beinn Eighe. Dogs are welcome. Kinlochewe also has two cafes.

The cairn called '305m' indicates the 1,000ft mark. Above, you can see how the quartzite, originally laid in flat layers on a sea bed, now dips fairly steeply towards Loch Maree. The path passes along the base of a crag, then turns up left to a cairn called 'Heather'. At the cairn called '460m' (about 1,500ft) you can see white marks the size of a thumb-print. These are the same worm-holes as at Trumpet Rock, but further in, away from the entrances. This 'pipe rock' layer is found all over Wester Ross.

The Conservation Cairn marks the high point of the path and has a fine view up to Beinn Eighe. The rotten quartzite pinnacles, called the Black Carls, are seen more clearly from Kinlochewe.

Their serrated outline gives the mountain its name, the Hill of the File.

Here the path turns right into a hummocky landscape of rocks and gravel – very much as the glaciers left it. You go down steps to pass a lochan, then reach another called Lunar Loch. The path now heads downhill – the descent not quite so steep as the climb.

Around the 305m cairn the heather is suddenly deeper, representing a narrow belt of mineral-rich bedrock as the path climbs a few steps to a knoll with a fine view along Loch Maree. Just below you can see the orange-coloured rock itself in the base of the Fossil Cairn. The fossils are in fact another sort of worm-hole.

The way descends to the left of the deep ravine of the Allt na h-Airighe. At the cairn called 'Ice Age', quartzite slabs show the scratches of the glacier that moved down the valley towards the left. The marks show most clearly on the fresh surface exposed by recent feet.

Back in the forest, turn left at a path junction where the Woodland Trail rejoins. Shortly, a short side-path on the right leads to a view point cairn built in layers of quartzite, sandstone and gneiss. The path drops through the sheltering trees to run quite close to the road below. At a junction, turn down left under the road by the bridge of the outward walk.

WHILE YOU'RE THERE

Queen Victoria stayed at the Loch Maree Hotel, where a small waterfall was named after her. A path leads up to it from a car park on the lochside road, or there's a longer forest walk from Slatterdale. Far above, the river divides into two branches (Grid ref: 884676). Locals suspect this unusual formation was an artificial means of improving the waterfall for the royal visit.

Into Scotland's Great Wilderness

*A pleasant walk around Loch Kernsary
and down the Ewe.*

DISTANCE 6.5 miles (10.4km)   **MINIMUM TIME** 2hrs 45min

ASCENT/GRADIENT 250ft (76m) ▲▲▲   **LEVEL OF DIFFICULTY** +++

PATHS Mostly good, but one short rough, wet section, 3 stiles

LANDSCAPE Moorland and loch side

SUGGESTED MAP OS Explorer 434 Gairloch & Loch Ewe

START/FINISH Grid reference: NG 857808

DOG FRIENDLINESS Close control on moorland and tracks carrying estate traffic

PARKING In Poolewe, just up B8057 side street

PUBLIC TOILETS At start

As you walk inland from Poolewe, you're entering one of the largest empty areas in Britain. Turn left instead of right at Kernsary Farm, and you can walk for two full days before you reach any road.

Great Wilderness

On the slight rise before Loch Kernsary, you get a surprise view right into the heart of this mountain wonderland. At the back of the view is A'Mhaighdean, The Maiden, Scotland's most remote mountain. It takes half a day's walk to get to this hill from anywhere. That walk will be along the edges of long dark lochs and under some very large crags. Beinn Lair has a quartzite cliff with an evil north-face gleam that's 3 miles (4.8km) wide, as big as the north face of Ben Nevis, but a whole lot less visited.

Behind A'Mhaighdean is An Teallach, called The Forge because of the cloudy vapours that stream across its semicircular ridge. That ridge has great lumpy towers to scramble round, 3ft (1m)-wide ridges to walk along and an edge that if you fall off, it will take about four seconds before you land on anything at all.

All this belongs to a gentleman from Holland called Paul van Vlissingen. In 1993 he signed an agreement with the Mountaineering Council of Scotland that first set out the principle of responsible access for all. Deer stalking restrictions would be only on days when deer stalking was actually taking place – a step forward when walkers were sometimes threatened with high-velocity rifle fire from August to February. The estate also undertook not to build any new landrover tracks. As a result, business here is carried out on foot, by boat and by pony. This Letterewe Accord became the foundation of the new century's access legislation.

Rights of Way

The paths used on this walk are, as it happens, established rights of way. Even so, you'll notice a sudden change near the head of Loch Kernsary. The first part of the path has been rebuilt by the National Trust for Scotland, using their members' annual subscriptions. One new member pays for about 2ft (60cm) of path. At the edge of National Trust land the path repairs stop abruptly, mid-bog.

In Scotland, no one is obliged to build or maintain footpaths. The surprising thing, if you walk all of these walks, is how many people are doing it anyway. Paths in this book are looked after by charities such as the John Muir Trust, by Scottish Natural Heritage and Forest Enterprise, by private landowners in Argyll and Atholl, by regional and community councils and groups of ordinary walkers.

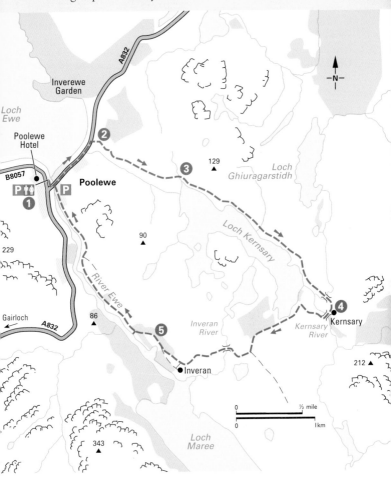

WALK 46 DIRECTIONS

1 A kissing gate beside the public toilets leads to a path that crosses the Marie Curie Field of Hope to the main road. Turn left to cross the bridge over the River Ewe and then head all the way through the village. At the 40mph derestriction sign, there's a white cottage on the right. Beside it, look for a tarred trackway that has a Scottish Rights of Way Society signpost for Kernsary.

2 Follow the track over a cattle grid to a new track that forks off to the left. After 50yds (46m), keep ahead on a path with a wall on its left. It passes through a kissing gate into Cnoc na Lise, the Garden Hill. This has been replanted as a community wood with oak and birch trees. Another kissing gate leads out of the young wood. The good, reconstructed path runs through gorse and then under a low-voltage power line. It crosses a low spur to a fine view of Loch Kernsary and the remote, steep-sided hills of the Great Wilderness, then goes over a stream to the loch side.

WHAT TO LOOK OUT FOR

The River Ewe may be short, but it's very full of salmon. As well as stony piers for anglers, you'll see artificial rapids where partial dams force the water into a central channel. Salmon will lie up in the pools below, waiting for rain to fill up the river, instead of proceeding immediately into Loch Maree.

❸ The path follows the left-hand shore of the loch, passing through patches of birch scrub. After a stile, near the loch head, it suddenly deteriorates, becoming a braided trod of boulder and bog. Once past the loch head, slant to the left down a meadow to find a footbridge under an oak tree. Head up, with a fence on your right, to join a track beside Kernsary farm.

WHERE TO EAT AND DRINK

The Poolewe Hotel was the original village inn. It has a restaurant, with fine sunset views (across the car park) and offers lighter meals in the bar/bistro (children are welcome, but not dogs). Opposite the car park you will find the Bridge House Coffee Shop and Gallery.

❹ Turn right, through a gate. Follow the track past the farm, to a culvert crossing of the Kernsary River. This becomes a ford only after heavy rain. If needed, you will find a footbridge 70yds (64m) upstream. After crossing, turn right on a smooth track. The new track bears left, away from Loch Kernsary towards the hollow containing Loch Maree. After the bridge over the Inveran River is a gate with a ladder stile. Signs welcoming responsible walkers (and even cyclists) reflect the principles of the Letterewe Accord. Soon come the first views of Loch Maree. The driveway of Inveran house joins from the left and the track starts being tarred.

❺ At a sign, 'Blind Corners', a green track on the left leads down to the point where the narrow loch imperceptibly becomes a wide river. Return to the main track and follow it above and then beside the River Ewe. It reaches Poolewe just beside the bridge.

WHILE YOU'RE THERE

One of Scotland's greatest gardens lies beside the Great Wilderness. In 1862, the Gairloch Mackenzies found themselves free of feuding Macleods and MacDonalds and turned their attention to gardening. Osgood Mackenzie planted trees to create shelter belts against the salt winds, improved (or rather, created) the soil using vast quantities of seaweed hauled up from the beach by basket, and found that the mild western climate would grow exotic plants from Chile and South Africa. Now managed by the National Trust for Scotland, Inverewe Garden is one of Ross-shire's most surprising and popular attractions.

Right: Inverewe Garden, Poolewe, (Walk 46)

Farigaig Forest and Loch Ness

*Overlooking Loch Ness and past the home of
a different monster, the Beast of Boleskine.*

DISTANCE *4.25 miles (6.8km)* MINIMUM TIME *2hrs 15min*

ASCENT/GRADIENT *700ft (213m)* ▲▲▲ LEVEL OF DIFFICULTY ✦✦✦

PATHS *Waymarked paths and tracks, no stiles*

LANDSCAPE *Hillside of mixed woodland*

SUGGESTED MAP *OS Explorer 416 Inverness, Loch Ness & Culloden*

START/FINISH *Grid reference: NH 522237*

DOG FRIENDLINESS *Keep on lead for short stretch past Easter Boleskine*

PARKING *Forest Enterprise car park*

PUBLIC TOILETS *At start*

With so many fine sights in Scotland, it's a shame that such large numbers of people take the trouble to see one that doesn't exist. The first encounter with the Loch Ness monster was back to the 6th century AD, when St Columba was crossing the River Ness. One of his companions was attacked by a water beast. When the saint ordered it to go away, it did. The onlookers, pagan barbarians whose friend had already been eaten, promptly converted to Christianity. The account was set down 100 years later by Adomnan, an abbot of Iona. It sounds suspiciously like an earlier incident from the life of a different holy man, St Martin of Tours, and also like a story about how Christianity took over a site where human sacrifice had been offered to a river god.

Later confirmation came during the Lisbon earthquake of 1755. A shock wave, freakishly magnified along Loch Ness, sent breakers crashing against the shore at Fort Augustus — clearly Columba's monster was still down there disturbing the water.

The Beast of Boleskine

Authentic sightings of a rather different monster did, however, take place in the early 1900s. Finding it fashionable to be Scottish, Alexander Crowley changed his name to Aleister and bought the nearby hall to become the Laird of Boleskine. In his time, he was known as 'The Beast of Boleskine', the 'wickedest man alive'. He identified himself with the Great Beast described in the final book of the Bible, the seven-headed monster that was to battle with the angels at the end of time.

In pursuit of his precept 'do what thou wilt shall be the whole of the law', he debauched minor film stars, when given the opportunity, betrayed his friends and became an alcoholic and heroin addict. At Boleskine, as he studied his magical books, the sky darkened at midday so candles had to be lit, and the lodge keeper went mad.

We might take the darkening of the sky as a normal Scottish summer raincloud, but we can still see the rowan trees his neighbours planted to protect themselves from his dangerous magical influence.

LOCH NESS

Apart from seducing his neighbours and brightening the Inverness-shire scene with various exotic mistresses, Crowley contributed to local life by prankishly reporting to the Society for the Suppression of Vice the prevalence of prostitution in Foyers (where there wasn't any). He also made an impassioned plea against the plan to enclose the Falls of Foyers in hydro-electric water pipes.

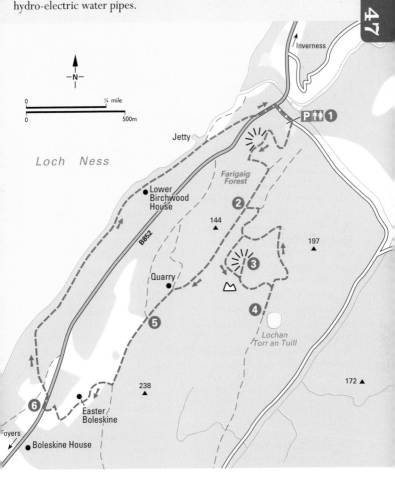

WALK 47 DIRECTIONS

1 From the car park follow yellow waymarkers uphill near a stream. After 100yds (91m), a path on the right has a yellow-top waymarker. After a bench, the path contours briefly then turns up left, to a higher viewpoint. It then turns back sharply left and descends on earth steps through a little crag to a forest road. Turn right for 200yds (183m).

2 Turn up left on a footpath with more yellow waymarkers. The path has a low, heavily mossed wall alongside as it bends up to a higher forest road. Turn right and walk for about 150yds (137m) until you reach a sharp left-hand bend. Turn off right here, on a small footpath walking through an area of small self-seeded trees, then go steeply up to the left underneath mature trees. At the top, bear left along a little ridge,

WALK 47

before dropping gently downhill to a fine viewpoint.

3 Return for 100yds (91m) and bear left down the other side of the ridge. The path now descends steeply until it reaches a forest road. A sign indicates Lochan Torr an Tuill, near by on the left, with a picnic table.

4 Return along the forest road, past where you joined it. It climbs gently and then descends to the sharp right bend where you turned off earlier – the waymarker says 'to Car Park' on the side now facing you. After 150yds (137m), at another 'to Car Park' waymarker, turn left down the path with the low mossed wall to the forest road below (Point **2**). Turn left, past a red/green waymarker. The track kinks left past a quarry.

5 Where the main track bends right, downhill, keep ahead on a green track with a red/green waymarker. It emerges from the trees at a signpost. Follow this down to the right towards

Easter Boleskine house. Green waymarkers indicate a diversion to the left of the house, to join its driveway track below. Follow this down to the B852.

6 Turn right for 50yds (46m). Below the left edge of the road is a tarred track. Turn down a faint path between the trees to cross this track, with a blue waymarker leading into a clearer path beyond. This passes down to the right of electricity transformers. At the foot of the slope, the main path bears right with a blue waymarker. It runs above the loch shore and joins a gravel track just below Lower Birchwood House. At a tarmac turning circle, an overgrown jetty on the left is great for monster-watchers. The tarred lane ahead leads up to the B852, with the car park just above on the right.

Strathpeffer and the Rogie Falls

From a Victorian spa to a salmon-leaping waterfall.

DISTANCE 10 miles (16.1km)	MINIMUM TIME 5hrs

ASCENT/GRADIENT 1,200ft (366m) ▲▲▲ LEVEL OF DIFFICULTY ✦✦✦

PATHS Waymarked paths and tracks, no stiles

LANDSCAPE Plantation, wild forest and riverside

SUGGESTED MAP OS Explorer 437 Ben Wyvis & Strathpeffer

START/FINISH Grid reference: NH 483582

DOG FRIENDLINESS Keep on lead for section past Loch Kinellan

PARKING Main square, Strathpeffer

PUBLIC TOILETS At start, Contin (Point ④) and Rogie Falls car parks

Stand on the bridge at Rogie Falls between July and September, when the river's fairly full, and you might catch a glimpse of a leaping salmon. It's a thrilling sight to see a 3ft (1m) long fish attempting to swim up against the force of the water. Eventually it'll make it, or else discover the easy way round – the fish ladder carved out of the rock on the right-hand side. But if you'd been here 200 years ago, that single salmon would have been a dozen, even a hundred.

The Rise and Fall of the Salmon

Salmon was once food for the taking. You went down to the river and took as many as you could eat. Smoked above a peat fire, it was a staple winter food. Farm workers even used their industrial muscle to demand that they shouldn't have to eat salmon more than three times a week.

Today, however, wild salmon are heading for extinction. The last decade saw the catch in Scotland's rivers shrink from 1,200 to 200 tons due to netting in the estuaries, and in their feeding grounds around the Arctic pack ice. Angling clubs have bought up and discontinued estuary netting rights but the international community squabbles on about the Arctic drift nets and now parasites and disease from fish farms pose a new danger.

Seven Ages of a Salmon

Egg, fry, alevin, parr, smolt, salmon, kelt – these are the seven ages of the salmon's life. For one or two years it behaves like a trout, hanging in the still water behind a boulder, waiting for food to float by. But then its scales become silver and it turns downstream, totally altering its body chemistry to enable it to live in salt water.

Return of the Salmon

Four or five years later, now called a salmon, it returns. We don't know how it navigates from Greenland back to the Cromarty Firth. Once there, it identifies the outflow of the Conon by the taste of the water and works its way upstream to return to the patch of gravel where its life began.

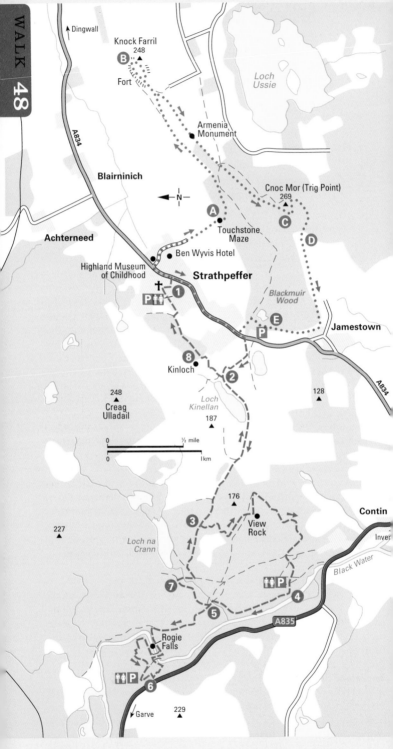

Dingwall

Knock Farril
248
▲
B
Fort

Loch
Ussie

A834

Armenia
Monument

Blairninich

← N →

Cnoc Mor (Trig Point)
269
▲
C

A
Touchstone
Maze

D

Achterneed

Ben Wyvis Hotel

Highland Museum
of Childhood

Strathpeffer

Blackmuir
Wood

P

Jamestown

E

P

1

8

Kinloch

2

A834

Loch
Kinellan

128
▲

248
▲
Creag
Ulladail

187
▲

0   ½ mile

0   1 km

176
▲

Contin

3

View
Rock

Inver

227
▲

Loch na
Crann

Black Water

7

5

P

4

A835

Rogie
Falls

P

6

Garve

229
▲

WALK 48 DIRECTIONS

1 Head along the main road towards Contin. When you reach the edge of the town, turn right at a metal signpost for Garve then, at a bend in the lane, turn left, following another signpost.

2 Follow track to the left of Loch Kinellan. As it bends right, keep ahead up a path beside tall broom bushes to the corner of a plantation. Here you join a larger track leading into the forest. Continue for 0.5 mile (800m) until it reaches a signpost.

3 Turn left for View Rock on a good path with green waymarkers. At View Rock, a side-path diverts to the right for the viewpoint, then rejoins. After a long descent, ignore a green path off to the left and follow green waymarkers downhill. At a forest road go straight over beside a signpost. The path crosses two more forest roads to Contin Forest car park.

4 At the end of the car park, pick up a wide path, 'River Walk'. Where red waymarkers turn back right, keep ahead on a rougher path with deer head markers. It bends up right beside a stream to a forest road. Turn left, signed 'Garve', and in 80yds (73m) bear left, heading slightly downhill.

5 Go on for 600yds (549m), when a small track on the left is signed 'Rogie Falls Bridge'. At its foot, cross a spectacular footbridge below the falls and

WALK 48

turn right, upstream. The path has green waymarkers and after 0.25 mile (400m) bends left, away from the river. It crosses rocky ground to a junction. Turn up right, to Rogie Falls car park.

6 Leave the car park through a wooden arch and follow green waymarkers back to the bridge. Retrace the outward route to Point **5** and turn sharp left up another forest road. It leads uphill to where a much fainter track crosses.

7 Turn right down the smaller track to pass between obstructing boulders, to a signpost. Turn left, signed 'Strathpeffer'. After 600yds (549m) it reaches the signpost at Point **3**. Keep ahead and retrace the outward route to Point **2**. Turn left on the tarred lane, which becomes a track. At Kinloch house bear right, then turn left through a kissing gate, with a second one beyond leading into a plantation with a signpost for Strathpeffer.

8 Follow the main path ahead until you see Strathpeffer down on the right. At the next junction bear right down the wood edge and turn right into town. The street on the left leads past a church with a square steeple, where you turn down right to the main square.

Cnoc Mor and Knock Farril

A grassy ridge walk above Strathpeffer to a vitrified fort.
See map and information panel for Walk 48

DISTANCE *5.5 miles (8.8km)* MINIMUM TIME *2hrs 30 min*
ASCENT/GRADIENT *950ft (290m)* ▲▲▲ LEVEL OF DIFFICULTY ✦✦✦

WALK 49 DIRECTIONS
(Walk 48 option)

From the car park, turn left down the main street towards the Ben Wyvis Hotel. Pass the hotel grounds and turn right, up a steep lane. It becomes a track; where this bends left, keep ahead up a field edge path towards the edge of the woods. Cross a stile and turn left to Touchstone Maze, Point **Ⓐ**.

The maze shows the rocks of this part of Scotland. If you've done Walks 40 to 46 in Wester Ross, you will find some more Torridonian sandstone here. From the top of the maze, an avenue of stones leads up and to the left. Ignore a path forking up to the right, and keep ahead to join a track at a waymarker. This runs to the left, keeping the same level through a gate with a stile where it leaves the woods. It continues level at first, then rises gently to a four-way signpost in a col. Turn left up a slope dotted with conglomerate rocks to the hill-fort of Knock Farril, Point **Ⓑ**. The first knob of ruined stonework on the left shows the vitrified rocks, thought to be caused by a fire that destroyed the fort's wooden palisade.

Return to the four-way sign and keep ahead for Cnoc Mor. The path passes a bench and follows the ridge-line above. A sculpture with three faces was a gift from Armenia to local schoolchildren who raised money after the earthquake there in December 1988. At the next col keep ahead through a kissing gate and over a stile, signed for Cnoc Mor. Under the pines a path, with a fence on its right, leads over a preliminary knoll and up to the trig point (Point **Ⓒ**).

Go down alongside the fence for another few steps before turning left on an overgrown track. This spirals round the hill to a signpost pointing towards you. Here a path on the right contours round the hill to another signpost. Keep ahead for Jamestown on a small, overgrown path. At the forest edge, turn down left, follow a fence past felled trees and cross a stile on the right (Point **Ⓓ**).

Continue downhill just inside the wood to pass houses at the edge of Jamestown. At a waymarker the path bends right to follow the wood's foot. After 650yds (594m) the path forks, with the right-hand branch running under pines to a car park (Point **Ⓔ**). Walk through here to the access road and follow this out to the main road. Turn right and walk down the hill on the pavement into Strathpeffer.

WALK

50

River Islands of Inverness

An Inverness town walk of riverside, seaside and canalside.

DISTANCE 7 miles (11.3km) **MINIMUM TIME** 3hrs

ASCENT/GRADIENT 197ft (60m) ▲▲▲ **LEVEL OF DIFFICULTY** ✦✦✦

PATHS Smooth and wide, no stiles

LANDSCAPE City and foreshore

SUGGESTED MAP OS Explorer 416 Inverness, Loch Ness & Culloden

START/FINISH Grid reference: NH 664447

DOG FRIENDLINESS Forbidden on Tomnahuirich and Whin Island – use alternative routes suggested in directions

PARKING Pay-and-display in Bishop Street, south of cathedral

PUBLIC TOILETS Whin Park and beside Inverness Castle

WALK 50 DIRECTIONS

Head downstream, with the river on your right and cathedral to your left, passing opposite the castle. Stay on the left-hand bank past a road bridge (it leads to the tourist information centre). Pass The Glenalbyn into Huntley Street, to a suspension footbridge.

WHERE TO EAT AND DRINK

Near the start of the walk, The Glenalbyn is a former 1700s coaching inn. It serves snacks, but does not welcome dogs. Dunbar's Hospital today houses a small, late-opening café.

Cross this, to the foot of Church Lane. At the other end of this short street is Dunbar's Hospital, a handsome building from 1688 and now a community centre and café. Return to the river and continue downstream, with the water on your left. A cycleway leads under the ugly concrete bridge of the A82. Turn left across the grey-girdered Waterloo Bridge, built in 1896, then right on Anderson Street and continue alongside the river, under a railway bridge.

Continue along the streets nearest the river, passing two branches of the Gael Force Marine Megastore. Beyond it you regain the river as it opens into the Beauly Firth. Behind a pumping station, a side-path leads to a beacon at Carnac Point. This has a fine view of the estuary and Kessock Bridge.

Continue along the shore to the old ferry slipway – you'll notice the corresponding slipway on the opposite shore. A sea wall path ahead runs above a seaweed expanse, where at low tide you will see curlews and sandpipers. After a level crossing, the path passes between salt pools to the Caledonian Canal.

On the right, lock keepers' cottages and a lighthouse mark the canal's entry into the salt water. Your route turns left, past the wide Muirtown Basin (on your right). After a swing bridge, the canal rises through a set of locks.

INVERNESS

WHAT TO LOOK FOR

The 130 bottlenose dolphins in the Moray Firth are the world's most northerly population. The narrows under Kessock Bridge are a common dolphin-spotting location. Those with binoculars might also spot seals, porpoises and whales.

Follow it for another 0.75 mile (1.2km) to a gate, with a swing bridge visible ahead.

Those with dogs must continue along the tow path to this swing bridge, those without can turn off left just before the gate, on a tarred path. Bruce Gardens ahead runs to the left of the wooded hill of Tomnahuirich Cemetery. A gate between white pillars lets you in. The cemetery is closed at night and dogs are forbidden.

For the most atmospheric path up, bear right inside the gates, then left on to a path under a lime tree. This joins a track at its hairpin bend. Go round left to rediscover the path above a red granite cylinder with urn. After 50yds (46m), turn left up a rhododendron tunnel. The path winds up the steep end of the hill, with several flights of steps. Across the top of the hill runs a gravestone avenue, dipping into a turning circle and ending at a war memorial with a fine view.

Return to the turning circle and turn right, down a track that bends back around the hill. At the prow of the hill, turn left

down steep steps to exit from the cemetery close to the swing bridge (if the gates ahead are locked, head left for 170yds (155m) to larger ones).

Turn right to the swing bridge of the Caledonian Canal mentioned earlier, but don't cross it. Just before it, turn left along the nearside tow path. (Those with dogs must at once fork left off the path here to follow the waymarkers of the Great Glen Way.) After 0.5 mile (800m), the River Ness appears below. Turn left on a path that runs past a rugby pitch to a footbridge to Whin Island. Again, dogs aren't allowed in this park.

Turn left on any path along the island, passing to the right of the ornamental pool to a path with the main river close by on the right. At the island's end is a footbridge which leads back to the left-hand bank of the river.

Turn right, downstream. This is again the Great Glen Way, where dogs and their owners rejoin the route. A tarred riverside path leads to a white suspension bridge. Cross to the first of the Ness Islands and turn left. At its end, another footbridge leads to a second island, and at the end of that, a further footbridge leads to the other bank of the river.

Turn left to continue downstream for another 650yds (594m). A final footbridge leads back across the river, with the cathedral 0.25 mile (400m) downstream.

WHILE YOU'RE THERE

Inverness Museum and Art Gallery is just up from the information centre. Next door is the castle. For an almost guaranteed dophin sighting, cross Kessock Bridge to North Kessock's WDCS Dolphin and Seal Centre. You can also hear them via hydrophones. (June–Sept, free admission)

Walking in Safety

All these walks are suitable for any reasonably fit person, but less experienced walkers should try the easier walks first. Route finding is usually straightforward, but you will find that an Ordnance Survey map is a useful addition to the route maps and descriptions.

RISKS

Although each walk here has been researched with a view to minimising the risks to the walkers who follow its route, no walk in the countryside can be considered to be completely free from risk. Walking in the outdoors will always require a degree of common sense and judgement to ensure that it is as safe as possible.

- Be particularly careful on cliff paths and in upland terrain, where the consequences of a slip can be very serious.

- Remember to check tidal conditions before walking on the seashore.

- Some sections of route are by, or cross, busy roads. Take care and remember traffic is a danger even on minor country lanes.

- Be careful around farmyard machinery and livestock, especially if you have children with you.

- Be aware of the consequences of changes in the weather and check the forecast before you set out. Carry spare clothing and a torch if you are walking in the winter months. Remember the weather can change very quickly at any time of the year, and in moorland and heathland areas, mist and fog can make route finding much harder. Don't set out in these conditions unless you are confident of your navigation skills in poor visibility. In summer remember to take account of the heat and sun; wear a hat and carry spare water.

- On walks away from centres of population you should carry a whistle and survival bag. If you do have an accident requiring the emergency services, make a note of your position as accurately as possible and dial 999.

COUNTRYSIDE CODE

- Be safe, plan ahead and follow any signs.

- Leave gates and property as you find them.

- Protect plants and animals and take your litter home.

- Keep dogs under close control.

- Consider other people.

For more information visit www.countrysideaccess.gov.uk/things_to_know/countryside_code